Leading the Team Organization

Issues in Organization and Management Series
Arthur P. Brief and Benjamin Schneider, *Editors*

Employee Ownership in America:
The Equity Solution
Corey Rosen, Katherine J. Klein, and
Karen M. Young

Generalizing From Laboratory to Field
Settings
Research Findings from Industrial-Organizational Psychology, Organizational Behavior, and Human Resource Management
Edwin A. Locke, editor

Working Together to Get Things Done
Managing for Organizational Productivity
Dean Tjosvold

Self-Esteem at Work
Research, Theory, and Practice
Joel Brockner

Implementing Routine and Radical
Innovations
A Comparative Study
Walter R. Nord and Sharon Tucker

The Outsiders
The Jews and Corporate America
Abraham Korman

Organizational Citizenship Behavior
The Good Soldier Syndrome
Dennis W. Organ

Facilitating Work Effectiveness
F. David Schoorman and Benjamin
Schneider, editors

Aggregation and Disaggregation in the
Social Sciences
Revised Edition
Michael T. Hannan

Future of Organizations
Innovating to Adapt Strategy and Human Resources to Rapid Technological Change
Jerald Hage, editor

The Lessons of Experience
How Successful Executives Develop on the Job
Morgan W. McCall, Jr., Michael A. Lombardo, and Ann M. Morrison

The Invisible Powers
The Language of Business
John Clancy

The Processes of Technological Innovation
Louis G. Tornatzky and Mitchell Fleisher

Pygmalion in Management
Productivity as a Self-Fulfilling Prophecy
Dov Eden

Service Management and Marketing
Managing the Moments of Truth in Service Competition
Christian Grönroos

Meanings of Occupational Work
A Collection of Essays
Arthur P. Brief and Walter R. Nord

Applying Psychology in Business
The Manager's Handbook
John W. Jones, Brian P. Steffy, and Douglas W. Bray, editors

The Essence of Leadership
The Four Keys to Leading Successfully
Edwin A. Locke

Leading the Team Organization
How to Create an Enduring Competitive Advantage
Dean Tjosvold and Mary M. Tjosvold

Leading the Team Organization

How to Create
an Enduring Competitive Advantage

Dean Tjosvold
Mary M. Tjosvold

LEXINGTON BOOKS
An Imprint of Macmillan, Inc.
NEW YORK
Maxwell Macmillan Canada
TORONTO
Maxwell Macmillan International
NEW YORK   OXFORD   SINGAPORE   SYDNEY

Library of Congress Cataloging-in-Publication Data

Tjosvold, Dean.
    Leading the team organization : how to create an enduring
competitive advantage / Dean Tjosvold, Mary M. Tjosvold.
        p.   cm.
    Includes bibliographical references and index.
    ISBN 0–669–27972–2
    1. Work groups.   2. Industrial organization.   3. Leadership.
I. Tjosvold, Mary M.   II. Title.
HD66.T54   1991
658.4′ 02—dc20   91–24664
                                                                           CIP

Lexington Books
An Imprint of Macmillan, Inc.
866 Third Avenue, New York, N.Y. 10022

Macmillan, Inc. is part of the Maxwell Communication
Group of Companies.

Printed in the United States of America

printing number

1   2   3   4   5   6   7   8   9   10

To Margaret Tjosvold, our mother,
and Dale Tjosvold, our father,
who led and nurtured
our first team

Contents

Preface ix

Acknowledgments xv

1 Teams and Leaders   1

PART ONE
Challenging the Status Quo   9

2 Confronting Leadership   11

3 Leadership
A Special Relationship   27

4 The Team Organization Model   39

PART TWO
Establishing the Team
Organization Framework   59

5 Storming and Forming the Management Team   61

6 Involving Middle Managers and Supervisors   71

7 Reaching Out to Employees and Unions   85

8 Forming Employee Teams for Innovation
and Commitment   101

PART THREE

Achieving Synergy 121

9 Task Forces and Project Teams 123

10 Leader Development Teams 143

11 Partnership across Organizations 157

12 Developing Your Team Organization 169

Appendix: Guides for Action and Pitfalls to Avoid 177
Notes 187
Index 193
About the Authors 197

Preface

Leading the Team Organization addresses the most inspiring and daunting leadership challenge: how to get people with diverse personal styles, vested interests, educational training, allegiance, and cultural backgrounds to work together to accomplish goals in such a way that they are committed to continuous improvement in themselves, their company and community.

Leaders call on us to find a common ground, inspire a shared vision of a better future, make us feel special and powerful, and show us how we can accomplish our common purposes. They are the architects of the teamwork that gets extraordinary things done. Leaders united people into productive, protective hunting and gathering societies 60,000 years ago, organized the energy and skill of thousands to build pyramids 5,000 years ago, and galvanized the moral courage to end slavery 150 years ago.

Our Challenges

We need much moral courage, unity, and organization today. Leaders are needed to help companies regain market share and self-confidence. North American automakers have since 1974 steadily lost domestic market share. Increases in productivity in the United States have slowed dramatically, and—except in the banking, telecommunications, and railroad industries—are near zero in the service industry.

The quality of our products and services is suspected. After spending eight years in *Time*'s Tokyo office, Edwin Reingold was "stunned" by the decline in service in the United States: "To a returning American grown accustomed to the civility and efficiency of modern Japan, the U.S. seems to have become a quagmire of bureaucracy, ineptitude, mean spirit and lackadaisy. . . . the repatriate is appalled and depressed by the lack of efficiency and of simple courtesy and caring."[1]

Doubts about our organizations are particularly troubling because a productive economy underwrites the employment opportunities and strong society that make individual fulfillment possible. In 1986 32 million Americans were below the poverty line; according to a Ford Foundation study, 63 million (nearly one in every four Americans) will be by the end of the century.

Indices of our social and psychological well-being also reveal disturbing trends. One out of every eighteen American adults (10 million in total) suffers from depression, with the highest rates for people between the ages of twenty-five and forty-four. Adults born around 1945 are ten times more likely to report they have had a serious depressive episode than seniors born around 1910, even though seniors have had many more years of opportunities.[2]

Young people show other disturbing sides of poor mental health. According to the National Center for Health Statistics, people ages fifteen to twenty-four are dying at a faster rate from accidents and homicides than people of any other age group below sixty-five. The third most frequent killer for young people is suicide. In Canada, suicide is behind accidents as the major cause of death for young people ages five to nineteen.[3] Results from the National Assessment of Education Progress in 1986 confirmed fears that many students are not developing the skills needed for employment in the twenty-first century. Only 7 percent of seventeen-year-olds, for example, had the advanced science skills needed to perform well in college-level science courses.

The family is under attack. Every year since 1972 more than a million children under eighteen years of age have been involved in a divorce. From 1980 to 1988, the number of children living with a single parent increased from 20 percent to 24 percent, and the number of births out of wedlock increased from 18 percent to 22 percent. Family income improved marginally from 1980 to 1988, but that is because more married mothers worked (the portion increased from 54% to 64%), including a jump from 41 percent to 54 percent in the number of working mothers with children below age three.

Deep divisions threaten the unity and strength of American society. In 1980 the average ratio of a CEO's salary to a blue-collar worker's was

25 : 1; by 1990 the ratio had climbed to 91 : 1. Unemployment for blacks is twice that for whites, and the discrepancy between black and white teenagers is growing. In 1990, 23,000 black men were enrolled in New York State colleges and universities, but there were 24,000 black men in New York state correctional facilities. Inequality is gaining ground worldwide. Many poor countries are getting poorer without much notice. In 1986 total World Bank aid to African nations was $2.9 billion; in 1986 U.S. government aid to Iowa farmers was $3.7 billion.

Our Need for Leadership

High-tech and low-tech manufacturing and service companies and organizations that educate and socialize our young and serve families and communities are calling out for leaders. We need leaders to help us join forces to confront uncertainties and take charge of threats. But we have found too little leadership.

We have found people to blame. Management blames poor quality and service on unskilled, uncaring employees. Surveys suggest that employees blame managers and became increasingly mistrustful of them during the 1980s; whereas employees want respect, recognition, and honest communication more than job security, but they believed they got less respect, less recognition, and less honesty.[3]

We have tried to escape from the social disarray. People have quit jobs, families, and communities rather than revive them, and they have tried to isolate themselves from others. A 1989 Gallup poll found that while a majority of Americans (54 percent) in 1990 expected to be better off in a year, only 25 percent expected that the country would be. Increasingly people have come to rely on the "self." The "me" generation thought that it could find fulfillment independent of others but instead found loneliness.

Blaming and escaping exacerbate our dilemmas for they further divide leader from follower and followers from each other. How can leaders forge meaningful, long-term teamwork when people are alienated from them and each other?

Common images and myths make people reluctant to take up the challenge of leadership. Leaders are thought to have a mysterious quality of charisma to garner power and to push their agenda despite the resistance of a short-sighted majority. They single-handedly rescue the company from the brink of disaster while others fiddle-faddle. Many managers doubt that they can live up to such expectations. Managers who try fall far short of such noble heights.

Leadership Is a "We" Thing

Leadership is special and noble but also very human and knowable. It is based on fundamental values of respect, caring, and achievement. Leaders reach out and inspire people to fulfill their potentials. They bring us together to find our common ground and accomplish our shared aspirations.

Leadership is not something done by one to another, but what people do together. Together leaders and followers envision a better future, feel united behind this common purpose, empower each other to perform, explore opposing ideas to solve problems, and celebrate and reflect on their achievements. *Leading the Team Organization* outlines how leaders and followers can together confront the suspicion that divides them and create a united, empowered company that serves its people and customers.

Using the Book

Leading the Team Organization articulates a model that summarizes our knowledge about leadership and teamwork to guide the reconstruction of our organizations. Wanting to work as a team is insufficient. The desire to be part of something greater than oneself, to make a difference with other people, to have a credible leader, and to have an inspiring, common vision are built into us and are very strong today. But we need useful knowledge about how to work together to turn these motives into concrete steps to construct the team organization.

Leading and participating in a team organization are full, emotional realities. Yet discussing relationships and teamwork can seem abstract and elusive. The team organization model and the leader's role in developing it are general frameworks that you can apply in many industries and settings.

We use an extended case study with characters and dialogue to tie the ideas down to situations and to show how the ideas can be applied. The company is fictitious, but the scenes are based on actual people and situations that we have encountered as employees, managers, business owners, consultants, researchers, and educators. The leader and people at Merchant Development & Construction, Inc. confronted real obstacles that require competent, persistent action to overcome. However, you and your organization may be more distracted by short-term issues, more skeptical, and less willing to experiment than people at Merchant. You and your organization may have to be more patient and courageous to overcome barriers and work as a team.

This book supplements previous work by the authors and in particular builds upon Dean's *Team Organization: An Enduring Competitive Advantage* (Chichester: Wiley, 1991), *The Conflict-Positive Organization: Stimulate Diversity and Create Unity* (Reading, Mass.: Addison-Wesley, 1991), and *Working Together to Get Things Done: Managing for Organizational Productivity* (Lexington, Mass.: Lexington Books, 1986). *Working Together* combines theory and research to understand interdependence and interaction in organizations. *Team Organization* uses this knowledge to develop an action-oriented model. *The Conflict-Positive Organization* shows how managing conflict contributes to spirited, productive teamwork. *Managing Conflict: The Key to Making Your Organization Work* (Minneapolis: Team Media, 1989) describes how a company uses conflict to revitalize its teamwork. Readers highly interested in a treatment of the research and theory behind this book may consult these books. References cited in this book may also help readers pursue specific issues.

Leading the Team Organization is both research-based and action-oriented. In addition to our research and writing, we have since 1976 collaborated in developing our family business so that it is in 1991 a successful, diversified $10 million company specializing in innovative facilities for elderly and handicapped persons. We have experienced the excitement, challenges, and obstacles to creating a first-class team organization. We invite you to join us and trust you can use this book as a guide for becoming a focused, high-performance team company.

Acknowledgments

We have taken the lead to write this book, but like other leaders we have relied on many people to accomplish our goal. Morton Deutsch and David W. Johnson have guided our two-decade journey to understanding interdependence and making knowledge about relationships accessible to those who work and manage our organizations. We have built the book upon the ideas and research of Chris Argyris, Bernie Bass, Dov Eden, Richard Field, Fred Fiedler, John Gardner, Bob House, Paul Goodman, George Graen, Rick Guzzo, Dan Ilgen, Dick Hackman, Jim Kouzes, Patrick Laughlin, Joe McGrath, Barry Posner, Vic Vroom, Phil Yetton, Gary Yukl, and many other capable leadership and group scholars.

We are fortunate to have worked with many open-minded, insightful managers who questioned our thinking and challenged us to develop our ideas fully. Bob Heywood, Jim Halco, Jeremy Jarvis, and Elsie Manley-Casimer, in particular, served as team organization leader models and critiqued earlier drafts of the manuscript. Jenny Tjosvold contributed to our research and writing and along with Jason, Wesley, Lena, and Colleen creates a most loving, lively family team.

1

Teams and Leaders

Not the cry, but the flight of the wild duck leads the flock to fly and follow.

—Chinese proverb

Leadership appears to be the art of getting others to want to do something that you are convinced should be done.

—Vance Packard, The Pyramid Climbers

Leaders and followers have choices about how they work and live together. You can view your organizational world in one of three ways:

Cooperative Team. You are part of a team committed to a common cause in which you help and are helped to be as effective and fulfilled as possible. You can get close to your colleagues and depend upon each other for support, encouragement, and information. You and employees form project teams to combine expertise and join task forces to explore problems and conflicts and to implement solutions that further mutual benefit. You feel united and loyal to your team and company.

Competitive Outdoing. You are in competition with your coworkers in a struggle to win; your success is measured against the performance of others. You should strive to feel like a winner, not a loser. You and your colleagues feel uncomfortable getting close and have difficulty trusting and depending upon each other. You work to develop your own resources to make yourself more valuable than others; you create solutions you believe solve important company issues and press others to accept them. You have a strong drive to prove you are more worthy than your peers or have given up on yourself as a loser.

Independent Work. You are alone; you should mind your own business and take pride in doing your own job well. You and your co-workers are reluctant to get close and believe that showing a desire to depend on each other scares people away and suggests an inability to cope with the job. You make sure you have the abilities and resources to do your own job. Although you protest when others interfere with your job and responsibilities, you willingly let others solve company problems. You feel isolated at work and look for human involvement off the job.

When presented with these choices, leaders and followers have little trouble identifying the advantages of a cooperative team. Many will say that they want teamwork, perhaps mixed with some competition and independence. But intentions and ringing speeches at annual meetings are insufficient. The issue is whether employees know their leaders' intentions, trust their integrity to follow them through, and whether leaders have the competence and savvy to put the cooperative team organization in place. Too many managers are ambiguous about what they want, get distracted by other priorities, are tempted into forcing their way, and are unable to manage the conflict and openness that team organization demands.

We have written this book to help you clarify your intentions and credibly communicate them to your team. We will convince you why the first option, the team organization, should be your choice. Hundreds of studies conducted in different settings with different tasks and different kinds of people, when taken together, indicate that people are productive and innovative as well as personally enhanced and fulfilled in cooperative, spirited teamwork.[1]

Competitive striving and working alone for independent ends, while at times useful and other times inevitable, have not demonstrated superiority over the cooperative team approach, although some studies suggest that they might be productive on simple tasks completed in a short period of time. For the long term, sustained motivation and complex problem solving demanded by contemporary organizations, the cooperative approach is going to get you where you want to go. Competitive outdoing and independent work are much more useful when they are contained within a more general cooperative framework.

Creating a team organization, while it gives much, takes much more than good intentions; it requires integrity, credibility, and vision. Organizational leaders—chief executive officers, presidents, strategic business heads, division and department managers, team leaders—must have a conceptual understanding of team organization, take risks to experiment with team procedures and practices, and work cooperatively with their boss, peers, and subordinates. They must teach employees about team organization and together have the courage and persistence to develop lively, spirited teamwork.

Team Organization

In a team organization, people are excited about the company's vision and want to serve its customers. They are in ongoing dialogues about how they can get their jobs done and make continuous improvements. They readily ask for assistance and feel free to speak their minds. They respect and appreciate each other as people and as contributors; they also directly challenge each other's ideas and positions. They want everyone to feel powerful, valuable, and included, not just those in the top positions. They forgive slights, misunderstandings, and opposition.

They realize that their variety of perspectives and training are needed if the company is going to flourish. Confronted with complex internal problems and customer demands, they form task forces and project teams of diverse people; they open-mindedly listen to opposing positions; they hammer out recommendations that make sense from a number of perspectives. They relish the give-and-take of discussing issues; they work to make sound solutions that deserve their commitment. They take pride and celebrate their individual and company achievements.

In the team organization, managers and employees are committed to their vision. People understand how their own efforts fit into the objectives of their department and the goals of their company. They believe that this vision unites them. They and their bosses and coworkers establish cooperative, congruent goals and rewards so that they can be successful together. They feel powerful and confident that they have the technical skills and interpersonal abilities to combine their resources to accomplish tasks and move toward attaining their goal. They explore problems by exchanging information and discussing opposing views openly to dig into issues and to create solutions. They reflect on their experiences to celebrate progress and learn from conflicts and mistakes. (See Figure 1–1.)

Teamwork is part of the organization's approach to getting things done. The organization as a whole envisions, unites, empowers, explores, and reflects. Groups believe that they share a common vision with other teams and individuals; they have cooperative goals, complement each other, discuss problems, and strengthen their work relationships.

Team Organization Model

FIGURE 1–1
Team Organization Model

The Team Organization Leader

Leaders work so that people have a common, inspiring vision of the organization's mission, feel united behind it, are empowered to realize it, feel confident to speak out and explore opposing positions to overcome obstacles, and reflect upon their progress and take corrective action to achieve their business objectives. More fundamentally, leaders take the initiative to nurture people and their relationships by constructing the team organization needed to achieve a mission.

Leaders recognize that the team organization is the most valuable of competitive advantages. Efficient technology is copied, lucrative markets draw competitors, profitable products lose their appeal, but a team organization continues to introduce new technologies, find new markets, create new products, and improve service to clients. Teamwork updates the mission and keeps it current.

How can leaders take the initiative to develop the team organization? They can use the team organization model. The model describes both the ends and the means for creating the enduring advantage of spirited teamwork.

Envision

Leaders refuse to be bogged down by the need to perform mundane tasks and respond to short-term crises. They rise above this by challenging the status quo and envisioning a more productive and fulfilling way to work together. They understand why working as a team will benefit them and the company. The team organization is rational and sensible as well as visionary.

Leaders speak credibly about the nature of productive teamwork. They have shrugged off worn-out notions about teamwork and leadership and have read and considered our current knowledge about leadership. Leaders articulate their understanding and belief in team organization and help employees learn and appreciate the meaning of teamwork.

Unite

Leaders inspire a shared conviction about the value of teamwork and the need to invest in developing the team organization. They work with people so that they see how working as a team generates shared rewards. They show how a team organization encourages innovation, improves profits, and benefits stockholders, which in turn makes employee jobs more secure and prestigious. Working as a team helps individuals meet needs to achieve, to belong to something larger than themselves, and to feel accepted as worthwhile and important. Teamwork does not suppress people but instead helps them express their individuality.

Empower

Successful leaders walk the walk as well as talk the talk. In working with individuals and groups, they demonstrate they are taking risks, practicing new ways of working, and modeling the way. Although far from perfect, they show they are learning the practical skills and procedures to structure, observe, and intervene to empower others to work together as a team. They emphasize that everyone should be learning and improving their skills in leading, working in teams, and managing conflict. They support training and development programs for individuals and groups. They know that a team organization is only successful to the extent that individual members are convinced of the value of their contributions.

Explore

Becoming a team organization is much more than following a recipe or a script. The best information system to help people collaborate, a compensation program that recognizes market realities but also leaves people feeling they are united and have been fairly treated, and the most practical forums for discussions must be worked out so that they fit the people, situation, organizational culture, community, and industry. A toy marketing company is not going to be organized identically to a university.

People will have opposing views about the many decisions necessary in creating a team organization. By discussing them openly and directly, they can explore the issues more deeply and create solutions that are useful and practical.

Reflect

Constructing the team organization is a journey, not a destination. It requires ongoing attention in which people continually upgrade and improve their teamwork. They honestly take stock of their relationships, diagnose problems, and give and receive feedback so that they are dealing with frustrations and conflicts.

Leaders encourage people to persist in overcoming old habits and developing new skills and ways to work. There are forces working to reassert the status quo and divide people. Successful leaders recognize that developing teamwork and working together require courage, heart, ongoing experimenting, and continuous improvement.

Managers have characterized successful leaders as far-sighted, inspiring, knowledgeable, sensitive, empowering, supportive, and challenging.[2] When leaders create a team organization, they demonstrate these characteristics to employees, and this lets employees demonstrate these characteristics to leaders and to each other.

The Book's Structure

To create a viable team organization, leaders must (1) gather the courage and understanding to confront the competitive-independent milieus of most organizations; (2) work with employees so that they are convinced that teamwork is to their advantage; and (3) put teamwork to work to achieve synergy up and down and across the organization.

The book has three corresponding parts. The first part, "Challenging the Status Quo," argues that leaders must confront popular ideas, myths, and fears about leadership and recognize that leadership is a joint responsibility and endeavor. The possibilities of integrated leadership and barriers to change in organizations and leaders are discussed in chapter 2. Chapter 3 argues that understanding leadership as a special relationship is a realistic, helpful lesson. The team organization model in chapter 4 specifies the nature of an effective leader and other relationships.

Part two, "Establishing the Team Organization Framework," describes how leaders can work with employees so that they understand and are committed to working as a team. Chapter 5 shows how leaders can discuss and debate team organization with their team, and chapter 6 describes procedures and processes that help a large group of managers understand and commit themselves to working together. Chapter 7 suggests ways to approach union and employee leaders to change the traditionally adversarial relations of labor and management. Fostering teamwork among employees can change a collection of individuals into a supportive, innovative group committed to both the company and employee learning (chapter 8).

The third part, "Achieving Synergy," details how managers and employees can use teamwork to integrate their perspectives to solve problems and develop their leadership and organization. Chapter 9 explores well-structured, diverse task forces and project teams, which are valuable vehicles for organizational decision making. How to implement collegial support teams to bring managers together to learn to be team leaders is the subject of chapter 10. Companies increasingly recognize the need for leadership across organizations, and chapter 11 suggests how team organization can be applied to this need. Team organization is not a quick fix to be forgotten as the next fad is tried. Chapter 12 reviews major steps for continuing to build and strengthen your team organization. Finally, the appendix summarizes major points made in the book by identifying guides for action and pitfalls to avoid.

PART ONE

Challenging the Status Quo

Leadership is such a vital and rich idea that developing the confidence and abilities to lead can be most perplexing. Managers get distracted and fail to use their opportunities unless they have a clear idea of what leadership is and how they can lead. In chapter 2, we see how one manager is confronting his challenge to be a leader. Chapter 3 argues that leaders are the builders of open, dynamic relationships in which they and their employees feel directed, united, and empowered. Chapter 4 describes the team organization model that specifies the nature of effective relationships between leaders and followers and among employees.

2

Confronting Leadership

The person who grabs the cat by the tail learns about 44 percent faster than the one just watching.

—Mark Twain

"**H**ow are you going to take advantage of your leadership opportunities, Brian? How are you going to make a difference?" Martin Sager asked. Brian Lowe was, for the first time, thoroughly enjoying his promotion to Vice-President, Property Management, Merchant Development & Construction, Inc. Brian, Martin, and the two others at the table, Karim Sandu and Heather Rubin, had formed a study group when they all took an executive management program from the local university. Through the rigors of working full-time and taking six courses in a year, they had become friends. Three years later, Brian's promotion was seen as a joyful reason to be together.

Martin's questions reawakened an aching, disturbing feeling in Brian that celebrating with his friends had eased. Brian could not admit fully to such a feeling, much less put his finger on its causes. He thought he was concerned about his relationships with his boss and his peers. They could be tough and unforgiving, and they also made sure you remembered that developing and constructing big projects is a risky business. Yet they weren't mean; he was surprised at how much humor there was at their meetings and how gentle they were with each other. They seemed to respect each other's turf and have a "If you don't cross me, I won't cross you" way of working. He thought he could fit in, but that did not erase his ambivalence.

He remembered feeling tied into a knot when Charles Sutherland, his boss, talked about how Brian had always been a leader and leadership is what the Property Management Group needs to give it a vigorous, competitive, entrepreneurial spirit. He had to strain to say something about looking forward to the challenges. He usually liked it when people called him a leader, but now that term loomed large.

Being with his friends made the pressures seem less formidable and more manageable. "We haven't decided whether to move to the west side of town or buy a summer villa in southern France," Brian replied to Martin with mock thoughtfulness.

"The first opportunity should be to buy us all dinner," Karim joined the fun. "Remember, you are here in your new job because we have been there for you!"

"I thought leaders were supposed to inspire the troops not scheme how to upgrade their lifestyles," Heather said.

"I'm just trying to get an executive perspective on life," Brian said. He turned serious and told them about his ambivalence and the burden of being a leader at Merchant. The Property Management Group (PMG) was demoralized and considered the dumping ground for people who didn't have the dynamic risk-taking skills of the development group, nor the "get it done regardless" attitude of the construction group.

His friends were well aware of Brian's private self-doubts. He had developed a "whiz kid" image for his successes in developing suburban industrial parks, but he had lost it, or at least much of it, on the ill-fated South Yellowstone Companies (SYCO) project. Everyone said it could have happened to anyone, but he couldn't help feeling that the failure and the money the company had lost were still talked about in the hallways. Being asked to take a management position, even though it was a top one, in the Property Management area only confirmed these suspicions. The failure of SYCO was something he would have to live with for as long as he stayed with Merchant. He would still look back occasionally and wonder, "How could I have been so stupid . . . so blind?"

"The Property Management Group sounds like it needs to be revitalized with more entrepreneurial spirit," Martin said. "But this is old news. You were telling us that years ago."

"True, but somehow it is much more 'my' problem since I'm in charge," Brian said.

"I bet people are pretty fed up with all that talk and those slogans about becoming a dynamic, excellent company," Martin commented. "I can see their heads nodding and their eyes rolling. What I want to know is what are you going to do?"

"You didn't get his job for something to do, but to do something, right?" Karim offered.

Brian was engaged. Later he would realize that they were helping him focus on his fears and anxieties for the first time. "Didn't we learn that a leader is flexible and does what the situation requires?" But he knew as he spoke that his response was lame. He did not have a clear direction for himself and his division.

"So you're going to wait and let the situation dictate—now that is a way to establish yourself as a leader with credibility, integrity, and vision," Heather said.

"I can just see people lining up to follow someone who exudes that kind of confidence and direction," Karim teased.

"Let's get back to how he is going to spend his money. What kind of haircut and suit will fit his executive image?" Martin laughed. "I think he's prepared to answer that."

"There's not too many answers around," Brian said. "Things don't seem as simple as they do in a textbook." Brian began to talk freely, and things bubbled to the surface for the first time. He could feel himself getting trapped into Merchant's top management syndrome of talking daring but playing it safe. "We talk about competitive edge and innovation, but everyone protects themselves and each other. We ask cotton ball questions of someone making a proposal to make it appear that we are a hard-nosed team digging into issues."

"You guys have to protect each other's fancy salaries and life-styles," Karim remarked.

"But we are also competitive as well," Brian continued. "We do curry the favor of Charles and try to show him we are better than the others, but not in a 'throw it in the other guy's face' way."

"Gentlemen's competition in close quarters," Heather said.

"I can see how it can be difficult to develop the team organization we talked about in our courses," Martin said. "Getting these people to work together doesn't sound easy. It *is* lonely at the top."

"The other VPs are outgoing enough, but, no, it isn't your basic support group," Brian said. "There is friendliness but also a 'better watch your backside' attitude."

"How about your own people?" asked Karim.

"Tons of stuff to do." Brian was relieved to turn away from the nebulous speculation about how he was going to create a team. "We've got a lot of properties to manage, and with the market as it is we think most of our growth and profits are going to have to come from managing what we have rather than building new projects. We have not been careful in how we are spending our maintenance dollars. So we are beginning a program of preventive maintenance that we think will eventually save us a great deal of money and hassle. I decided I would go out and visit some of the sites, and traveling certainly eats up the time. And, of course, there are memos to write, meetings to attend." Brian felt stronger as he addressed the concrete tasks he had in front of him. Through courses, conferences, and his work, he identified with excellence in property management.

"Are you having fun?" Martin asked seriously.

Martin had again asked a question that stirred Brian. "It beats sitting around all day." Brian realized, though it would only be later that he would explicitly recognize it, that the activity was a relief from thinking about how he was supposed to be a leader transforming the property group. He liked the feeling of digging into a concrete task, getting something done, and proving himself. Navel-gazing and abstract planning were not his strong suits.

"I don't think you want the job dictating to you." Heather pointed out. "You are in charge, not the job."

"I thought we learned that we weren't supposed to take charge of our employees but empower them," Brian said.

"But empowering them does not mean depowering you," Martin observed. "Employees don't want dominance, but they do want leadership, direction, and vision from the top. Remember, we talked about how leadership is a relationship that goes two ways: they influence you and you influence them. It is only together that you and they can be powerful."

Martin's comments reminded Brian of the discussions they had on the importance of trust, cooperation, and teamwork. The terms had such meaning for them at the time, but their relevance for the property group was vague. "It is so tempting to use power much differently. I have so many chances every day to order someone around, tell them it's my way or the highway. And there's little they can do about it because I sign the checks."

"They could go to your boss," Karim suggested.

"So you think that is why I don't do it?" Brian teased. "But squealing could be very costly, and the boss almost *has* to support me."

"Have we forgotten the long term?" Karim asked. "Employees do nod their heads and do what they are told, but you pay later. They might quit, even if they stay on the payroll."

"I remember when we had this jerk for a boss, we banded together for self-protection," Heather said. "You should have heard the jokes about him at our Friday after-work beer nights. It got to be great when he barked out an order. We would say, 'Good idea' and pretend to comply and then laugh together when he was out of earshot. Poor guy, he never did figure out what hit him. I actually feel a little guilty now, but he seemed to want to make it him against us, and there were more of us."

"Scary," Brian said. "But our people are more loyal than that."

"We wanted to be loyal," Heather said, "but the boss made that impossible."

"Brian's not going to get in that jam," Martin said. "He's going to develop a team approach—cooperation and positive conflict in action. It will be beautiful to watch our ideas bear fruit at Merchant."

"Right!" Brian exclaimed with a smile. "We have action already, but beauty is still in the wings. We did have beauty in action in our study group."

The group happily reminisced about their experiences together. Somehow, no one was quite sure how, they had clicked and developed a bond. The open discussion, the direct support, the emphasis on learning were so fresh and invigorating. They knew that Martin was instrumental in their development, perhaps because he was not interested in projecting a corporate power image. He believed that personal relationships were of great value, argued that they should make the program a success for everyone, and was genuinely warm and interested in others. Once the group really experienced cooperation, the appeal and logic were irresistible.

On the drive home, Brian was relaxing in the warm camaraderie of his friends and thought how lucky he was to have peers who could appreciate and value his success. He was also contemplative, for he knew now was the time to bring what he could to his job. He did not want to look back and think he had just coped and gotten by. Nor would it be enough to fit in with his peers and look good to his boss.

Leadership, trust, cooperation, and positive conflict had become meaningful words to him; he had experienced their power in his study group. What was so liberating about cooperation was that it put self-interest in a new light. He had assumed that pursuing his interests was selfish, even mean, and that one should really try to be altruistic. Every time he heard the word cooperation he felt some guilt because he was not altruistic, but even more angry because selflessness seemed such an impossible standard. What "should be" seemed so far removed from what was.

But the study group's cooperation was different. They all openly pursued their self-interests—to get the assignments completed, to learn, to enjoy themselves, to know each other—together. If one group member knew about finance, that helped the rest of them learn. They actually cheered each other on: they wanted each other to succeed.

He had also assumed "cooperation" meant people sitting around all day being nice and agreeable. All these "motherhood" calls for cooperation put even more pressure on people to control themselves and their feelings. What resulted was papered-over harmony.

The study group's cooperation was not harmonious sameness but diverse individuality. Bringing together people with backgrounds in engineering, corporate management, social services, and finance made the group's discussions lively and spirited. At first people were upset when others disagreed and had a different perspective on a problem or a case. But as they worked together, they became more open-minded and trusting. Opposing perspectives were accepted as natural and productive.

Brian's study group reminded him of previous good experiences as part of a team. His wrestling teammates in college became fast friends through the ordeal of riding bikes in saunas to make weight, unending bus rides to meets, winning and losing matches. But his study group was his first group he had been involved in that focused on "business."

The insights into relationships that he developed in the study group affected his work style. He was at first embarrassed when his coworkers teased him about the executive program changing him; later he told them that, given its cost and demands, the program had better change him. He was more tuned into and less uptight with coworkers, especially concerning their quarrels, and he enjoyed himself and them more. He didn't feel trapped by disagreements; he could chose how he wanted to approach each conflict. What he noticed most was that he was less driven. He no longer felt the pressure always to prove himself, show he was right and had all the answers. He took the longer, broader view of things at work. His peers and subordinates told him that he was more approachable and open. He felt less compelled to control people and get them to do it "his way."

If only he had been tuned into relationships, then he would not have been so stubborn and closed-minded about the SYCO project. He would not have dismissed the possibility that two major clients might withdraw, and then he could have delayed or redirected the project before construction began. SYCO would have only been a disappointment, not a disaster.

His experience with these ideas about relationships helped him, and none too soon, develop a new way of living with his family. He realized that he was not really listening to his wife or managing his conflicts. He would usually tune out and try to appease his wife, Edith, by giving in. Or, if giving in seemed like too much, he would try to overpower and bully her. She tolerated his approach—"What do you expect when you marry a Lowe?" she would say to anyone who would listen—but she was not happy about it.

The insights were even more useful in his relationship with his son, Dereck. Brian could not accept that his son was not going to be the aggressive, outgoing sports hero he wanted. Dereck was a tender, even vulnerable seventeen-year-old who would rather practice his sax than play football. Brian realized with help from Edith and his group that his pressure and badgering were driving Dereck away. Now he was committed to developing his relationship with Dereck and to making it very clear that he loved and cared for him.

The trouble was that Dereck did not reciprocate quickly. Brian realized he would have to be disciplined and determined, and he was grateful that some warmth was returning to their relationship.

His insights were also useful when he came to realize that, despite his hopes and demands, Sarah, his daughter, was not at all interested in becoming a first-class musician and instead put her energies into sports, not education. He did not let that disappointment interfere with providing the support and encouragement she needed to make the most of her abilities.

These ideas about cooperative, give-and-take relationships now seemed so sensible and obvious that it was hard to image why they were so strange at first. Yet it was not so clear how he could apply his insights and translate the ideas to the Property Management Group at Merchant. Letting things take their course wouldn't work because Charles and the top management group had already established a much different way of working. He would have to manage his boss and peers so that they understood what he was trying to accomplish. Perhaps some day they would appreciate the team approach.

The larger challenge would be leading his division toward becoming a lively, spirited, productive team. That would be a legacy he would be proud of. It would not be easy.

By this point Brian, with his shoes off and feet up, was sitting in the big chair in the living room. His wife's coming out of the bedroom had disturbed his ruminating about the evening and his plans, but her warm "Hello, honey" and kiss were welcomed.

"You look like you had fun," she said. "It is good to see you relaxed for a change."

"Great time."

"Did Karim say anything about Norene's surprise party for Heather?" Edith and Norene, Karim Sandu's wife, often got together during class and study sessions. They had become friends and enjoyed their time together; they joked that their husbands would have to keep taking classes and meeting.

"I think he said something about the party being on," Brian answered.

"My husband, the fountain of information. I think I'll call Norene. What deep thoughts are you having?"

"Well, you know . . ." Brian stammered. "I guess I'm a little worried about my challenges as a leader of the Property Management Group."

"Oh, that. I don't think you have to solve all the problems yourself tonight. Why don't you save some for tomorrow and for others and go to bed now."

A few years ago he would have seen only the sarcasm in his wife's comment and became irritated, but now he said, "Good idea."

As he got up from the chair, he thought, "She's right. I don't have to create the team organization by myself now." And again he relaxed.

Getting Perspective on Leadership

Brian had worked hard for his promotion to Vice President of the Property Management Group, and he was determined to succeed. He knew he had to please his boss and fit in with his peers. The boss wanted him to shake up the department and make it less bureaucratic. Brian thought he could develop a direction and vision centered on making the division more entrepreneurial; if he did it right, the division could gain respect for its contributions to the bottom line. People in the division would develop a sense of urgency and importance about these possibilities. Although the day-to-day details seemed to take over his day, he had begun to talk about his plans whenever he had the chance.

Brian began to take a broader perspective by talking with his study group friends. He began to realize that, while he was acting a leader in formulating the mission of the business, he had virtually ignored leading in the sense of fostering the vital organization needed to accomplish the business vision. The division was supposed to be more entrepreneurial, but how people were to communicate and work together were not high on Brian's agenda. The employees assumed that they would continue to have the same kinds of relationships, though they watched Brian for any possible signal of an alteration.

Barriers to Leading a Team Organization

After celebrating with his friends, Brian was surprised that he had been blind to the opportunities to revitalize the organization. Yet in another way it was completely understandable that he had made this oversight. Merchant and many other companies are managed in such a way to dissuade people from taking on the challenge to create a team organization.

Task Single-Mindedness

Brian's boss would talk about making the company lean and mean, but he was much more comfortable dealing with business plans and strategy. He liked the excitement of pitting his wits against competitors in formulating strategy, and while he enjoyed talking to people, he seemed to have gone through life with few incentives or opportunities to examine his relationships and his personal management style.

Many companies are dominated by a single-minded focus on the technical and task-oriented aspects of business. It is not difficult for people in our culture to understand that for the company to prosper and for individuals to be successful things have to get done. A forest company has to cut down trees and mill them. But that there must be an organization and a set of relationships that need to be nurtured and strengthened for these tasks to get done effectively over the long run is not so widely appreciated.

Brian's own personal history reinforced this restricted emphasis on the task. Whether he was wrestling or studying, he accomplished his goals and took pride in his achievements. Such successes had lead him to focus on getting things done, usually by his own initiative. Although he had learned, despite the image of developers as rugged individualists, that putting together a new industrial park required much collaborative effort, he had to remind himself that as a manager he had to work with others. He still had not fully incorporated the idea that success as a manager would come as he created an environment that helped people work competently and together to get things done.

Competitive-Individualistic Climates

Companies that have the strongest work relationships invest and develop themselves as organizations. People who are working together find new and more effective ways to collaborate. The team organization has multiplier effects. On the other hand, managers and employees who feel distant and competitive find it difficult to break out of these dynamics; it takes two to establish productive cooperative work relationships. While cooperative organizations keep on improving, competitive-individualistic companies box themselves in.

In trying hard to fit in and be a part of the team of his peers, Brian feared "standing out." His peers followed the lead of Charles. Brian anticipated, even without explicitly reasoning, that if he began to talk about developing a team organization where people had strong personal relationships that allowed them to manage conflict and work together, they would at least raise their eyebrows in bewilderment. They might also worry that Brian was going to upset their world. Such attitudes would greatly increase the risks for Brian. If he succeeded, his peers might resent his upstaging them, and if he failed, his peers would let him take the heat and savor the "I told you so" attitude.

Brian's relationships with the people in the Property Management Group also made work on the team organization risky. In discussing his hopes for openness, trust, and working as a team, he could not help feeling a little embarrassed and vulnerable. Perhaps employees would dismiss him as "on a new idea" and "not doing his job." They might laugh at his "weak" style or be angry and sullen if he was unable to follow through.

Competitive-individualistic cultures, like other aspects of the status quo, have developed rationales and justifications. Competition is touted as a central component of the free market system and credited for the success of capitalism and the demise of communism. Recently managers have understood that their companies must develop a competitive advantage. Competition is widely thought to motivate, yet theorists from Adam Smith to Michael Porter have focused on the competition between organizations and have assumed that within organizations cooperation is required. Indeed, these theorists have argued that there should also be a great deal of cooperation between organizations, sometimes even between competitors in joint ventures and programs to enhance their industry.

Individuals develop defenses to justify their actions and frustrations in competitive-individualistic climates: "If you don't like the heat, get out of the kitchen," "Business is a jungle," "Work hard, party hard." These justifications, defenses, and habits make a team organization seem both ineffectual and threatening.

Ambiguities about Leadership

Leadership is a revered idea that provokes strong feelings and attitudes, but this richness confuses and pressures many managers like Brian. How could he be like those leaders who transformed their companies, bringing them back from the brink of disaster to health through the sheer charisma of their personality and the grit of their determination? He could buy into the image, he doubted he could pull it off.

Nor is it very clear how someone actually leads. Isn't leadership a mysterious quality that some people are born with, and others not? Brian, like many other managers, believed that leadership was something he did himself. It was natural for him, in the competitive-individualistic world of Merchant and in his own experiences, to think like that. People were expected to do their own job, and his job was leadership. He could by himself develop a general mission, although he would still have to "sell" this vision. Creating a team organization would have to be done with others.

Mentors in many organizations are misleading role models. We acquire much of our understanding of leadership by observing our own bosses and teachers. Breaking out of traditional leadership modes can seem very foreign and risky. It can even seem like we are challenging and attacking the bosses and teachers whom we have looked up to. We need the support of significant others to cope with the emotional demands of leading a team organization.

Ineffective managing is often blamed on the pervasive short-term orientation of many companies. But to companies dominated by task single-mindeness, competitive-individualistic climates, and ambiguous notions of leadership, developing a team organization seems complex and distant, and easily dismissed as impractical. People recognize that they will feel much more effective, at least in the short run, in getting a concrete task completed rather than in building a team organization. Buying a computerized press can seem much more practical than having people spend the day talking about their feelings. The more people avoid dealing with their relationships, the harder it becomes to discuss them, and the harder people try to get the job done despite working at cross-purposes. As a result, short-term crises management dominates.

The Courage to Challenge the Status Quo

Talking with his friends reminded Brian that developing a team organization is a legacy that will last. The value of a new business mission or new technology wanes with time, but investing in the team organization endures. A well-managed company creates new strategies and adopts emerging technology in its ongoing effort to form competitive advantages and remain a viable company. Brian was gaining perspective on how he could mobilize his challenge to the status quo at Merchant.

The Critical Value of Relationships

We all live in a network of relationships, and to a great extent our well-being and fortune depend upon these networks of family, friends, workers, and country. Our interdependence is so pervasive that we sometimes do not "see" it. Unfortunately, we often see it too late—after we have let the family split apart, moved away from friends, quit our job, or let our country divide against itself.

Fortunately, Brian learned the simple, but powerful lesson of the importance of relationships without undergoing an ordeal. His learning and experience with his study group had helped him see that he needed to invest in his relationships with Edith, Dereck, and Sarah. He spent time with them, took their perspective, and accepted them for who they were. He found to his surprise that he influenced them more after he stopped trying to control them.

Brian rejoiced in his family relationships, and his first thoughts in the morning were how lucky he was. Even getting ahead and making money were much more meaningful when he could share them with his family. He approached colleagues differently, and even these minor changes brought a freshness to his work life. He knew he could speak credibly about the value of relationships, and other people would be receptive because they were learning to value each other.

The traditional view is that success comes from a focus on the task, and that while strong relationships might be nice and psychologically valuable, they are not central to business. We now appreciate that it is through people that the information, knowledge, and ideas flow that are the lifeblood of organizations. We also know that the strongest motivators are other people, and that disrupted relationships undermine efficacy and effort.

Through people working together, problems are solved, new technology utilized, and innovations adopted. Relationships are not only important for the morale and commitment of employees, but also they are necessary for business success. There is no fundamental trade-off between developing relationships and getting the job done. Relationships and tasks go together; strong relationships are necessary for long-term success.

Discontent with the Status Quo

Competitive-individualistic climates are difficult to break out of because they undermine the joint effort needed to establish more successful relationships. They create discontent through undermining mutual support and assistance and fostering a pressure to "win" by oneself. While there are a few "winners," there are usually many more "losers." Even winning can seem very fleeting, and good only until tomorrow's competition.

In addition to people's frustrations and isolation, the competitive-individualistic climates do not deliver over the long term. Of course in the short term favorable markets and sheer effort can result in profit levels that make it appear that the company is doing well. But when a downturn comes, as it inevitably must, the bad habit of not working together will haunt the company.

The impersonal, competitive, and independent climates of most organizations have within them the energy and seeds of their own demise, but they also perpetuate themselves and obstruct the coordination necessary to change them. Capturing the frustration within them and channelling it into creating the team organization requires leadership.

In the next chapter we argue that Brian and his employees must develop productive work relationships with each other so that they feel united behind a common direction, empowered to act, able to explore various ideas to make decisions, and willing to reflect upon their experiences and conflict. Yet each relationship is different because it is an expression of the unique personalities of leaders and followers. Chapter 3 details the nature of these team relationships, and subsequent chapters describe how you can use these ideas to create a team organization.

3

Leadership

A Special Relationship

Leaders listen, take advice, lose arguments, and follow . . . I didn't turn the company around. I presided over it. The people in this company turned it around. I was the captain of the ship, but they were doing all the rowing.

—Irwin Fedries, President and CEO, Monolithic Memories

The reason we were so good, and continued to be so good, was because he [Joe Paterno] forces you to develop an inner love among the players. It is much harder to give up on your buddy than it is to give up on your coach. I really believe that over the years the teams I played on were almost unbeatable in tight situations. When we needed to get that six inches we got it because of our love for each other. Our camaraderie existed because of the kind of coach and the kind of person Joe was.

—Dave Joyner

"**Y**ou guys had me all fired up about being a leader and creating a team organization. Now I'm just fired up," Brian told Martin. "And I think I know who I can take it out on."

"What are friends for?" Martin remarked. "I suppose you're going to make me pay for lunch, too."

"Good idea!" Brian said. Brian had invited Martin for lunch to talk about his new job, especially the pressures and opportunities to be a leader. He told Martin that although his talk with the study group friends had him thinking about how to be a leader and create teamwork, he was not able to put it together.

"I try to begin the day thinking about how to be a leader, but everyone else seems to be interested in this memo, that meeting, buying a new computer system, you name it. There just does not seem to be enough time in the day. What am I suppose to tell these people—that I am not interested?"

"All those things sound like they need to be done," Martin agreed. "Telling your employees you're not interested in their concerns is not my idea of leadership."

"Even if I had the time, I don't think I'm up to being this dynamic leader. Remember when we discussed how leaders are supposed to be honest, visionary, credible, ethical, the list is endless?"

"Leaders are supposed to be consistent but flexible, directed but open-minded, confident but selfless, tough but soft . . . No problem."

"No problem other than paralysis. How am I supposed to have integrity and consistency? One of my managers, Lance, came into my office yesterday to complain about Calvin. So I listened to this for a while and just get burned up inside. Why is he going on and on when I've got a million things to do? I just cut him off in midsentence and told him I had to get ready for another meeting. This is the kind of nitty-gritty that leads me to not being credible."

"What did you do when Calvin came in to complain about Lance?"

"How did you know Calvin came in?"

"I've seen this 'tell the boss and get him on your side' game before."

"I felt guilty about not listening to Lance so I tried to listen to Calvin. Bye-bye consistency. I just don't have the time for the kind of garbage my managers bring to me."

"No one said leadership was an easy thing, but I think you're making it more abstract and grand than you need to. Didn't we decide that leaders create relationships in which followers see them as honest, competent, and credible and that the leader sees the followers in the same way?"

"Leadership is a two-way street, I remember that."

"So you want to develop good work relationships with your employees and among your employees. The leader's special role is to take the initiative in creating this team feeling and way of working."

"But you are throwing the burden back on me, and, frankly, I have enough to do," Brian replied.

"The leader takes the first steps," Martin responded, "but employees must also reciprocate and get on board. You can't force people to have strong working relationships."

"When am I suppose to have the time to do this?"

"Pay now or pay later. You have Lance and Calvin running to complain to you rather than to each other. Do you have time for that?"

"No time and no patience."

"The saying, 'If you don't have time to do it right the first time, when will you find the time to do it over?' applies to relationships. You have to live with your relationships whether they are good or bad."

"But I can't always succeed. Sometimes the relationship is not going to click."

"I'm not sure they have to click, and sometimes they are not going to work out. But you are credible and disciplined if you work to make your relationships strong."

"But I can't treat everyone the same."

Martin and Brian talked for some time about what treating people the same and being fair mean. It is totally unrealistic, they decided, that leaders should behave in the same way toward everyone. People, situations, tasks are too different to allow that. But leaders can be consistent by striving to develop mutually beneficial relationships. At times leaders are supportive, and at others times confrontational. At times they focus on the business task and other times on relationship conflicts. Yet their values of respect for other people and desire to create mutually beneficial relationships give them and their followers a feeling of integrity and credibility.

"What I really don't think I can do is develop this kind of relationship with my boss," Brian said. "He just doesn't have the kind of style that will let me open up to him and tell him my fears about my own leadership and my frustrations with his. That just won't go."

"But I think you have to try and go the second, even third mile to at least move toward a good relationship," Martin counselled. "You can't be preaching and trying one thing with your division and doing something very different with your boss. Whining about your own boss won't fly either. The more clout you have with your boss, the better for your managers. They'll forgive you, and they may even admire you if you try, but they'll get demoralized if they think you're not even trying to make progress. Your people will understand that you don't have total control. They know they can't control you."

"Tell me again that I don't have to sit around and be nice all day long to be a good leader," Brian urged.

"Brian, you not only don't have to be nice, you shouldn't be. You should be your honest self. Sometimes you are going to get angry and need to confront people for being careless and self-centered. Sometimes you are even going to make a mistake and just be wrong. One of the good things about being a cooperative leader is that you don't have to be perfect. You're all learning, experimenting, and taking risks together, and inevitably there'll be stumbles. But you are on each other's side and able to discuss difficulties, and that makes all the difference in the world."

Walking back to the office, Brian felt a sense of optimism and confidence that he could be a leader. Being a leader wasn't mysterious and abstract, but the very down-to-earth developing of relationships. Yet leading was still inspiring and challenging. How could he take the lead in strengthening his relationships with the division's managers? That would be a place to begin. But he also wanted to help his managers work together and approach his boss.

The Myth of the Successful Competitive Leader

Robert Helmreich and his associates investigated how differences in the desire to achieve affected individuals' success.[1] They proposed that the desire to achieve has three parts: competitiveness as the desire to win in interpersonal situations in which others must lose; mastery as the desire to take on challenging tasks; and work as positive attitudes toward working hard. To their surprise, they found that male Ph.D. scientists who were most successful as measured by citations of their work were high on mastery and work, but low on competitiveness. Competitive scientists apparently get distracted by attempts to outshine others and produce research that is more superficial and less sustained than less competitive scientists.

Subsequent studies confirmed the basic findings. Successful businessmen (as measured by salaries) in large corporations had lower competitiveness and higher mastery and work scores than less successful ones. Similarly, low-ranked competitive airline pilots, airline reservation agents, supertanker crews, and students were all more effective than highly competitive ones. Helmreich and his researchers were unable to identify any profession in which more competitive persons are more successful. Taking on challenges and working hard are not synonymous with competition. Indeed, it is when competitiveness is low that the desires for challenges and hard work result in success.

⟶ The Leader Relationship

Brian was coming to understand that leadership was not so much a mysterious quality that he might not possess. Leadership is creating productive work relationships. He could use his own experiences and strengths to forge relationships, and, as relationships are two-way, employees could bring their interpersonal skills and attitudes to bear.

Yet the leader relationship idea does not imply that leading is a simple quick fix. Forming productive work relationships under the stresses and pressures of contemporary organizations is not a one- or two-step affair. Developing the leader relationship is an ongoing journey that requires much from both leader and followers. But this relationship pays off in mutual respect, self-confidence, and achievement.

Developing the relationship between leader and follower is, as with other relationships, both simple and complex. It is simple in that it rests on a belief that the leader and follower are on the same side, that they can be successful together, and that their goals are cooperative. They must also be able to discuss their differences and negotiate agreements. Developing the leader relationship is complex because cooperative goals must be continually reinforced by a common vision, rewards, tasks, attitudes, and values, and because negotiation requires self-awareness, empathy, creativity, and compromise. Leader relationships must also be developed under the pressures of time and productivity in contemporary organizational life.

Obstacles of Unequal Power and Authority

The hierarchy of power and authority can make developing the leader relationship particularly challenging. As Brian discussed with his study group friends, leaders are tempted to use their power to demand their way. Because in the short term there is little an employee can do, the boss is left with the illusion that there are few if any consequences for his controlling and coercing. This kind of superior power can corrupt.

The superior authority of the leader can also disrupt. Managers sometimes turn the legitimacy to make decisions into a belief that they have, or ought to have, the competence to make all the decisions by themselves. Taken to the extreme, managers fall into the trap of barking out orders and making snap decisions when they clearly do not have the information or expertise to do so. They are intent on proving themselves right, and, by inference, everyone else wrong.

Unfortunately, the managers' very superiority of power and authority leaves them unprepared to appreciate the impact they are having on employees. Like Heather's former boss, they may not realize their employees have banded together for self-protection and revenge, and then they may never know what hit them. People with superior power are often uninterested in taking the views and perspectives of the less powerful who have little impact on them. Managers also have a number of employees to try to understand.

Employees help managers live in ignorance. They are reluctant to bring up "hot" issues that might irritate the boss for fear the boss will blame the messenger. Employees also take the short-term view and hope that somehow the problems will work out, but in the meantime they will keep their head down and collect their paycheck. They create a great variety of ways to cope, from looking for another place to work to dreaming about their next vacation destination. Alcohol and drugs are highly self-destructive forms of adaptation.

Employees' misconceptions about leadership also interfere. While they have incentives to figure out their boss, they often do not appreciate the pressures on their boss. The life of a boss may well seem much rosier and richer than their own, but in many organizations bosses must be on guard against rivals and mischief-makers, form alliances for self-protection, and cope with a difficult boss. Because of the years they have invested in the company, any misstep may seem very costly. And many bosses feel pressured to keep their frustrations bottled up for fear of revealing their shortcomings or worrying employees.

Employees are also trapped by the boss's superior authority. They also assume that the boss is in the position to know their ideas, feelings, and frustrations. They think to themselves or tell each other, "If the boss wanted to do something about my plight, then she would do something." Yet the boss may not even know that an employee is angry, let alone the reasons behind the anger. The boss may well assume that the employee would take the initiative if there was a problem.

Bosses and employees help each other avoid conflict and stay out of touch. Yet, their feelings of frustration and anger do not disappear. They fester, distort, and pollute until employees burst into anger or passively resign themselves to their fate. But everyone pays.

Beginning Steps

There is no inevitability that managers and their employees will have closed, conflict-avoiding relationships. Many employees respect their bosses as their mentors and learn a great deal from them. Managers, in turn, recognize the energy and creativity of employees, relish the give-and-take, and find nurturing younger employees most rewarding and affirming.

There are major pitfalls to avoid. Leaders who use their power to force their way, use their position to assert that they are always right and know the answer to every problem, and fail to take the perspective of employees are asking for trouble. But leaders do not have to do all of the relating by themselves. They can work with employees to develop a strong team organization relationship.

Chapter 3 outlines the characteristics of these relationships, and subsequent chapters indicate how they can be developed.

Research on Cooperative Leadership

Traditionally, researchers have investigated the ways managers persuade, direct, and influence employees. But the effects of any strategy depend upon the relationship the leader has with the employee. A command may induce compliance and commitment with one employee, but resentment and resistance with another. To lead requires employees who want to be led.

Cooperative Relationship

Recent studies document the central role the cooperative relationship plays in successful leadership. Recently 110 medical laboratory workers identified the extent to which their leaders had developed cooperative, competitive, or independent relationships with them.[2] Leaders who had cooperative relationships, results suggest, inspired commitment and were considered competent. Competitive and independent leaders, on the other hand, were seen as obstructive and ineffective.

In a follow-up study both managers and employees were interviewed on specific instances in which they worked together.[3] From the standpoint of both managers and employees, cooperative goals, in contrast to competitive goals, were found to improve the communication, exchange, and influence between them. This interaction, in turn, resulted in progress on the job and efficient use of resources, strengthened confidence in future collaboration, and created positive affect. Employees found independent managers obstructive.

The study also identified interactions that helped and interfered with productive work. In effective situations, leaders and employees assisted each other by sharing resources and expertise, integrated different points of view and ideas to solve problems, discussed issues to reach a mutually satisfying agreement, showed initiative, consulted with others, and followed proper procedures. Unproductive work was characterized by being unwilling to help and giving the task low priority, viewing the problem only from one's own perspective, refusing to discuss problems, strictly following job descriptions, ignoring advice, working in isolation, and failing to follow procedures.

Cooperative Power and Authority

The traditional view of power is that it is zero-sum: the more power the leader has, the less power employees have. The contemporary view sees power as expandable—the total amount of power can be enlarged so that leaders and employees both feel more powerful and more influential.

Kanter, an ardent champion of the value of power for organizations, proposed that employees prefer powerful managers who are able to protect them from unwanted interference and obtain organizational resources.[4] Powerful managers are also considered more confident and willing to be helpful.

Studies have documented that leaders and employees who develop cooperative relationships are able to put power into constructive use. In a variety of situations, compared to competitive goals, cooperative goals created higher expectations of assistance, more assistance, greater support, more persuasion, and less coercion, as well as more trusting and friendly attitudes in power relationships.[5] Evidence collected in various organizations indicates that these dynamics and outcomes of cooperation occur in ongoing relationships.[6] Within cooperative relationships, employees and leaders are able to exchange resources and be productive.

As with power, authority can be buttressed and made more effective when it is shared. Leaders who use a collaborative, participative approach to carrying out their authority were found to inspire commitment.[7] In contrast, both supervisors who want to control major decisions and supervisors who abdicate decision making responsibilities were considered ineffective and frustrating.

The participation of employees in solving problems and making decisions can improve the quality of solutions and the commitment to implement them.[8] However, a cooperative relationship is needed for employees to voice their opposing views, participate fully, and use the potential of shared decision making.

The consequences of managerial styles and strategies depend upon the nature of the relationship that leaders and employees develop. Cooperative relationships foster collaborative, effective influence, positive power, and authentic participation in decision making. Competition leads managers to use tough, forceful strategies that backfire.[9]

Successful leaders have various styles and personalities and flexibly use different ways to influence others. What they have in common are interpersonal abilities and sensitivities.[10] They develop strong, cooperative relationships within which they influence, are open to influence, and work productively with employees.

A leader without followers is not a leader. Leaders develop relationships in which they are seen as powerful, authoritative, farsighted, credible, capable, and trustworthy. These relationships also make employees powerful, farsighted, and trustworthy. Leaders flexibly use methods and procedures appropriate for the situation, but consistently pursue cooperative relationships.

Managing Your Boss

Employees not only can manage their boss, they must. While they may be tempted to blame the leader for not being more supportive, open-minded, and cooperative, such blaming does not resolve the issues. Ganging up on the boss and complaining to the boss's boss are strategies that give the impression that employees are competitive. These strategies will lead the employee to be labelled disloyal and untrustworthy, and too weak to deal with problems directly and openly.

Employees are part of the leader relationship and need to be involved in developing it. They must not think they are powerless, for they can help their boss understand the value of a strong leader relationship and work with the boss to realize it. Sometimes, of course, the relationship can be so difficult that employees give up because their boss is too unprepared and unequipped to develop open, cooperative relationships with employees. Remember, there are managers who have not read this book!

Structuring Relationships among Employees

Many leaders are tuned into the need to have good work relationships with their employees and can call upon their experiences and skills in working with others. Brian, for example, can bring insights and sensitivities he has learned from working with colleagues and study group members, living with his wife and kids, and from college, even childhood, experiences.

Particularly difficult and challenging is developing relationships among employees. These relationships, as subsequent chapters testify, are critical for leadership success and organizational effectiveness. In addition to interpersonal skills and sensitivities, leaders need a framework so that they can clearly communicate the kind of relationships they want established, how they are to be developed, and their own role in the process. Many managers do not have an articulated framework but only foggy notions about the nature of these relationships.

Towards a Dynamic Integrity

Brian had serious doubts that he had the confidence and abilities to be a leader. Maybe he would lead his team down a blind alley. Was he prepared to have people invest in doing it his way? Could he really be charismatic? He was also baffled at the many apparently conflicting demands on leaders. They should be flexible, yet consistent. They need to be confident yet not arrogant. They must be persuasive yet open-minded. They should be forceful, but responsive.

Brian's talking with his friends and reflecting helped him feel more comfortable and confident in his role as leader. He felt less divided and conflicted and could sense how he could work in a way that was congruent with who he was. Brian had begun to discover that he could use leadership as a team relationship to integrate apparent inconsistencies into a coherent way to lead.

Team organization leaders can integrate the values of productivity and people. A team organization is valuable and stimulating for people; it also facilitates the business mission, institutes a meaningful preventive maintenance program, and earns the respect of other divisions by contributing to the company's profitability.

Brian could also integrate his personal values and life with his work values and life.[11] He would not have to transform himself every night from office slave driver and autocrat to a father guilty because he both gave in too much and demanded too much. He could apply the skills and sensitivities he learned at home to the office, and what he learned at the office to home.

The nurturing of team relationships is the stable core of leadership. But this integrity is an open dynamic in which leaders and followers continue to grow and learn. The team leader relationship is not a straitjacket or rigid rules but involves values and sensitivities that can be developed and expressed in many ways. Team organization leaders and followers are always experimenting with new ways to work together.

The burden of leadership is not just on Brian, for leadership and teamwork are things that managers and employees do together. Brian and his employees, we argue, must build team relationships in which diverse people feel united behind a common direction, empowered to act, able to explore different perspectives to make decisions, and capable of reflecting upon their experiences and conflicts. Yet each relationship is different as it is an expression of the unique personalities of leaders and followers. The next chapter describes the nature of these team relationships. Subsequent chapters describe how you can use these ideas to forge your own leader relationships and teamwork.

4

The Team Organization Model

From the standpoint of everyday life . . . there is one thing we do know;
that man is here for the sake of other men—above all, for those upon
whose well-being our own happiness depends, and also for the count-
less unknown souls with whose fate we are connected by a bond of
sympathy. Many times a day I realize how much of my own outer and
inner life is built upon the labors of my fellow men, both living and
dead, and how earnestly I must exert myself in order to give in return
as much as I have received.

—*Albert Einstein*

To be only for oneself is to be almost nothing.

—*B. F. Skinner*

Brian woke early the next morning and sensed that it was going to be a good day. He felt both more alert and relaxed than he had in some time. As was his routine, he was enjoying drinking coffee and reading the newspaper before the rest of the family got up. He was glad Dereck came downstairs first.

"Good morning, Dereck," he said with genuine cheer.

"Hi, Dad," Dereck replied. "How does an old guy like you get up so early?"

"Habit mostly, I guess," Brian said with a laugh. "But I look forward to the day's activities."

"You like going to the office and having to do what everyone else wants you to do? That is not my idea of a good time."

"I enjoy it," Brian responded directly. "You're right, I have to do what other people want, but others do what I want, too. It's teamwork really, and when you can work as a team with people you respect and like, it's a great feeling."

"I'll play my sax, thank you," Dereck retorted definitely.

Brian decided to take his son's attitude as a challenge rather than as disrespect or a rejection of the business world. "But you enjoy getting around and jamming with your friends. You certainly enjoy your dance band."

"But that's different, Dad. We're helping each other express ourselves musically and emotionally, as well as make some money."

"We do that, too. We help each other express our ideas and feelings, help each other learn, support each other . . ."

"Feelings . . . in business."

"There's lots of feelings in business. The whole gamut from despair to exaltation, from anger to affection. If you do it right, working in a company is a great experience." Brian congratulated himself that he had been so direct with Dereck and had avoided getting huffy and irritated. He knew that he had not convinced his son of the intrinsic rewards of working with other people in a company, but he could see the wheels in Dereck's brain turning. He sensed that he was not too late and would eventually repair his relationship with Dereck.

He had meant what he said to Dereck, but he also knew that work was needed to realize the potential of Property Management to become a lively, supportive team. He felt emboldened, after talking with his study group friends and thinking about it, but that did not mean he had a plan. He could reread some of the articles and books, but perhaps first he would approach the people who reported directly to him.

Brian and his four department managers were meeting that afternoon to discuss the slow progress of the new preventive maintenance program. It was odd, he thought, last week he and the group had been thinking about how to turn up the pressure to get people's attention and motivation behind the program. This week he saw more clearly that the lack of team organization was interfering with progress. Yet he felt some anxiety about bringing up the subject. Was it because Lance Keegan, manager of operations-domestic, might be skeptical? Calvin Stone, manager of marketing, might even be upset. Or was it because he doubted he was ready to take the plunge, really up to the demands of creating a team organization?

His conversations with his study group friends, his wife, and his son had built up such a momentum that he knew he was going to begin. He also remembered that he would not have to do it all himself. He would rely on his managers and employees to help him create the team organization.

"I would like us to consider doing some work on how we and the division are organized," Brian began. "We can work better not just by working longer and harder but by working together. This preventive maintenance program is a good idea. We're frustrated because people do not seem to be pitching in to make the thing work without a lot of overseeing and pushing from us. We need to create a team organization, and I hope we can do it together."

Brian was surprised that they were so slow in responding, although he could see that they were considering and weighing what he had said.

Finally, Calvin spoke up. "Do you mean that we are going to be reorganized and restructured?"

Brian's answer that he wasn't planning to start moving people around the organization chart reassured Calvin but left him unsure about what Brian was driving at.

Anthony Lopez liked what he heard. "I think Brian is getting at that we should improve our relationships so that people are feeling together. 'We are in this together' sort of thing. Let's go for it."

Lance, surprised at how actually irritated he was at Brian's comments, tried to keep his feelings in check. He said, trying to sound funny but with the sarcasm showing through, "Go, going, gone, and we are out of here."

Wanting to encourage Lance to speak directly about his concerns, Brian said with a laugh, "We are going to be out of where? Out of our minds? Seriously, I'm not sure what you mean."

"I'm just showing my age," Lance said, grateful that Brian seemed to want to listen and not let him look foolish. "I guess I have heard so many fancy words by so many high-priced consultants that whenever I hear organization development my mind glazes over and a dark cloud appears."

Janine Fong, usually the most reluctant to join in teasing, laughed and said, "That's because Anthony has gone and created a cloud of dust."

Brian was glad that people were enjoying themselves, but he also wanted them to be serious. "Janine, what do you think of the idea of a team organization?"

"It doesn't sound bad certainly, but I would like to know more about what a team organization is," she said.

"I hope you don't mean everyone sitting around and being nice to each other," Calvin said. "We have business to do."

The group debated what a team organization meant. Anthony argued that good work relationships make good business sense. Lance argued that it would be a long, windy, and costly venture to become a real team. Janine wondered if the employees might not feel directionless. Calvin doubted that with the market changing so fast it was really the right time to be altering the organization.

"This is fun," Brian said. "I like to see you guys mix it up. How we work with other people is so important to us as people and to our organization that we have strong opinions about it."

"Opinions, yes," Lance said. "Knowledge you did not mention!"

"Do you have materials we can read on team organization?" Janine asked.

"I have some articles and a book or two," Brian said. "Would that help?"

"Send them to everyone," Anthony said. "Then we can discuss team organization next week."

"I hope this information won't interfere with our debate," Lance laughed.

"We haven't let knowledge interfere before," Calvin joked.

"I suppose Calvin is sore because we don't quote his marketing research studies," Anthony replied.

"Seriously, is there really good research behind this team organization idea?" Lance asked. "Or is it fancy words or a new bottle for outworn ideas?"

"There have been good ideas and a great deal of research for a while, but the instructors in my executive program said it is just getting put into a form that we can understand and use," Brian said. "But you can read for yourself. Let's follow Anthony's plan and read this week and discuss next week."

Driving home, Brian laughed to himself about the discussion about team organization. Laughing together and debating ideas were both therapeutic and honest. But he didn't want the sessions to degenerate into just a debate or a contest to see who could crack the most jokes. They had a serious mission to develop PMG and make it a place where they could all be proud and successful. That, Brian knew, could only come if they really did work together.

They had taken the first steps in developing their organization, and he sensed that they were going to have a good time along the way. He looked forward to dinner with the family and then the great fun of coaching Sarah's basketball team.

"Okay, class, have you done your homework?" Brian began the managers' discussion on team organization to a chorus of "I did."

"Good. Now as it is most important to identify who knows it best I have a short quiz," Brian said.

"Excuse me, sir" Anthony joined the fun. "I don't think seeing who is the best is consistent with operating as a team. I thought we were supposed to be united and have common goals, not competitive ones."

"I got carried away!" Brian said laughing. "I had copies made of the model; let me pass them out as a way to begin talking about it. Let's first see how far we can get in understanding it and thinking about whether we can use it. Perhaps at the next meeting we can critique the model."

Brian went over the five parts of the model (see Figure 1–1): Envision, Unite, Empower, Explore, and Reflect. These parts reinforce each other. Effective groups don't do just one of them well but all five. He suggested that each person study one part and give the group a definition.

After fifteen minutes of reading and asking each other a few questions, Calvin began. "The envision part has to do with where we are going: What is our strategy? What are we trying to accomplish? How would we like things to be different?"

"That includes not only our objectives but our vision of how we are managed. How we work together, in short, is our vision of the organization," Brian added.

"The unite part is getting us all together working for a common cause," Anthony said. "We should all see that where we are going will leave us all better off. We will all feel successful if we reach our business agenda, and all of us will be rewarded. We will either swim together or sink together."

"Empowering has to do with having the confidence that we can do it," Janine said. "The team needs to feel confident that it can be successful. We all know situations in which people aren't motivated because they don't think they can do it. So they sit around and complain. They need resources, of course, and trust that each team member will do his or her fair share. Poor teamwork is demoralizing."

"Explore is also an important step to team success," Lance said. "All groups must make decisions, and if they make good ones the group stays on track and gets the job done. Unfortunately, groups are tempted to latch onto the first solution that appears or the one the boss seems to want. Groups must be able to explore opposing positions and possible solutions to solve problems effectively. At least this part of the team organization comes to me naturally," Lance said.

Brian summarized reflecting: "Groups are not machines, but they need to examine and improve how they envision, unite, empower, and explore. Teams are either growing or declining. The vision needs to be updated to respond to changes. Conflicts must be managed or we run the risk of undermining unity and confidence in each other. Groups may be blind to new possibilities and use sloppy problem-solving methods. Ongoing learning should be high on the team's agenda."

"There is quite a bit in this model," Anthony said, "I think we need to discuss each part in some depth."

"Me, too," Brian said. "We studied it in my executive development course, but I find it useful to go over it. It seems like I keep picking up parts of it the more I study it. Let's all discuss each part and think about ways we can use it."

The Components of the Team Organization

Successful teamwork is both one thing and many things. There is no one step or hurdle that itself makes a team productive. Yet the different parts of teamwork complement and supplement each other. Teams that have a vision and feel united also have more confidence that they can be successful together, and they are better able to explore different points of views. Through their openness they look for ways to learn from their experiences and improve how they work together as well as how they can accomplish their business vision more effectively.

Teamwork is required up and down the hierarchy and across groups and divisions. People throughout the organization and committed to their common vision, believe they are united behind the vision, are empowered to work together to realize it, explore issues and decisions through debating opposing views, and reflect on their conflicts and progress to promote ongoing improvement.

Envision: What Direction?

> No wind favors him who has no destined port.
> —Michael E. deMontaigne

A clear, engaging direction is a central first step to developing a team organization.[1] All members are fully aware of the team's strategic plan, code of ethics, and organizational structure: They know what they are expected to accomplish and how they will work together to achieve it. They understand the importance of this vision for themselves and others, and they are committed to pursuing it. This vision motivates and directs them.

Visions must be created; they do not just appear. Effective leaders look beyond the everyday distractions of work to ponder the future of how things might be. Leaders are pioneers who challenge the status quo and are willing to risk failure to search for a better way.[2] Though not necessarily originators of innovations, they recognize good ideas and work to get them implemented. They challenge, experiment, and innovate.

Yet leaders cannot create the vision alone. They listen to employee concerns and ideas to help them create the group's vision. They enlist employees to help them mold the vision. They realize they cannot command commitment—they must inspire it. Leaders are "keepers of the dream," as Steve Jobs said, but they must inspire others to share this dream.

Ways leaders can create a shared vision include:

1. *Assess the team's vision.* Customers, industry experts, and competitors help team members examine the present strategy to assess its viability and risks.
2. *Reflect on the organization framework.* Team members discuss the nature of productive teamwork and compare their work relationships to the team organization model.
3. *Confront relationship issues.* Dealing directly with grievances and conflicts sets the stage for forging a common vision. It demonstrates management's dedication to building a team organization.
4. *Search for opportunities to initiate change, to innovate, and to grow.* Rather than wait for a crisis to hit, the team finds something that is "broken" it can fix. They break out of the routine and usual and consider their work an adventure to enjoy. Employees talk about their concerns about the business strategy, and about what bugs and annoys them about their jobs and their work environment. They let each other know what they want to change in the strategy and management of their team.
5. *Take risks and learn from mistakes.* People gather new ideas and try little experiments.
6. *Present a short vision statement.* A leader or task force evokes images and metaphors in describing the mission and organization framework for the company.
7. *Dialogue and include.* Team members discuss the vision, code of ethics, and corporate values so that the strategy and organization framework make sense to them.
8. *Update.* The team revises its vision in light of changes in and out of the group. It again hears customers' ideas and complaints, the predictions of industry experts, and reviews from the competition.
9. *Appreciate accomplishments.* The team celebrates its capacity to change and rewards progress toward its vision.

A newsletter prepared by a team members summarizes progress toward achieving the vision.

Unite: Are We Together?

United we stand, divided we fall.
—*Watchword of the American Revolution*

An effective vision convinces team members that they are united in a common effort. Sensing they are moving in the same direction, they communicate openly and understand each other. They realize they need the information, knowledge, ideas, support, and energy of others to get their jobs done and to contribute successfully to the company.

Cooperative unity cannot be taken for granted. Even having a vision does not guarantee it. Employees might believe that they should compete against each other to show the boss that they are the most committed to the vision. They may want to prove to themselves that they are better than others. Cooperative work at times seems impractical and costly. Employees would rather work on their own individual task rather than take the time from a busy day to coordinate. The costs of scheduling another meeting and rearranging vacation time are often very immediate whereas the benefits of working together to develop a new program are more distant.

Nor can unity be decreed. It is not enough for managers to talk about how employees should cooperate or to blame them for not cooperating. People must come to their own conclusion that what is good for one is good for all; success for one is success for all. Moreover, cooperative dependence needs to be a shared conclusion. One person can not cooperate alone. Everybody must see the positively related goals and be willing to work together to accomplish them.

People use various cues and information to conclude that they have cooperative goals. The levers managers use can include:

1. *Explore the team's vision.* All members know the purpose

and value of the vision. They understand that no one can
fulfill the vision alone; they must work together.
2. *Assign a task and ask for one product.* The team as a
whole is to develop a new product or solve a problem.
The manager wants team members to integrate their ideas
and develop one solution. Each team member signs off on
the team's output indicating that he or she has contributed
and supports it. Then the group assigns responsibilities to
members to coordinate different aspects of the solution.
3. *Keep track of group productivity.* All workers average
their individual output to form a group average for each
week. Each worker is responsible for keeping his or her
output up, and for helping others improve theirs.
4. *Promote group learning.* All group members are expected
to improve their skills in managing, selling, or operating
machinery, and to help each other learn. The manager will
chose at random one team member to demonstrate what
he or she has learned, and the team is rated on that basis.
5. *Praise the team as a whole for its success.* The manager
recognizes all members of the team, and their
accomplishments are written up in the company
newsletter.
6. *Reward individuals based on group performance.* Each
team member receives a monetary bonus based on the
team's success.
7. *Hold an unproductive group accountable.* Managers
confront failed teams and have them suffer some
consequence, rather than single out individuals for blame.
8. *Make the task challenging.* Team members will be highly
motivated to accomplish probable, but difficult tasks and
will recognize they need everyone's ability and support to
do so.
9. *Pledge to cooperate.* Team members begin meetings by
openly declaring that they will cooperate and work
together. Trust can be established when team members
believe that everyone has decided to promote common
goals and to reciprocate cooperation.
10. *Limit the resources to the group.* Team members realize
that as individuals they cannot each try to accomplish the
task; instead they must pool their resources.

11. *Assign complementary roles.* One employee is asked to record ideas, another to encourage full participation, another to be a devil's advocate to challenge common views, and a fourth to observe and to provide feedback to help the group reflect on how well it is working.
12. *Encourage team identity.* Teams devise and publicize their own name and symbol. Members focus on their common characteristics and backgrounds.
13. *Promote personal relationships.* Team members discuss their feelings and the values they consider important. "Small talk" about family and self develops personal, trusting relationships. Social gatherings such as Friday afternoon "beer busts" and Christmas parties encourage such interaction.
14. *Write a philosophy.* Team members develop their own value statement. These values emphasize that the members belong together, care about each other, and should be helpful "citizens." Employees recall stories and examples that illustrate the vision, values, norms, and unity of the team.
15. *Unite with other teams.* Group members understand how the effectiveness of other groups helps them accomplish their goals. Teams seek out ways to contribute to each other's success. They reject the short-term strategy of building cooperative unity by projecting another department as the enemy.

Empower: Can We Do It?

I never got very far until I stopped imagining I had to do everything myself.
—Frank W. Woolworth

Feeling united in a common effort contributes to developing confidence that the team can realize its vision. But feeling united is insufficient. Team members do not exert themselves fully unless they believe that they have the technical resources, organizational mandate, and the skills to combine their ideas and efforts successfully.

Empowering, like envisioning and uniting, cannot be done to people; they themselves must believe that they can do it.[3]

Teams are not islands. They need the organization's mandate, permission, and support to be highly effective. The company provides the new product team with the time, money, and other resources to do its job. Team members also must believe that management will give them approval to produce and market their product if it meets requirements. Without such expectations, team members feel "what's the point of trying?"

Believing that team members have the necessary technical skills and resources to reach the group goal is central to a sense of power and confidence. When the new product team members believe that together people have the research, development, industrial engineering, production, and marketing expertise to be successful, they are prepared to join forces in a common effort.

Interpersonal and social skills are also vital. Cooperative goals themselves do not result in productive work; people must actually work together effectively. Working together requires sensitivity, empathy, and confrontation. People should be aware of the feelings and needs of others and respond to them. They must exchange information and at times challenge each other's position and thinking. If a new product team believes that meetings will be unproductive and unhappy because of indifference or acrimony, they won't have much enthusiasm. Similarly, they need the opportunities of team meetings and gatherings to exchange and assist each other.

Individual responsibility and team accountability empower a group. Team members do not want members who are "free riders" and take them for "suckers" who will end up doing all the work. People avoid situations in which they suspect that they will be unjustly exploited. Team members want to divide the labor fairly and effectively. They feel a sense of personal accountability to complete their tasks so that other team members can complete theirs. They do their own jobs and whatever else it takes so that the team as a whole is successful.

Teams can follow these steps to empowerment:

1. *Relate the team's vision to the organization's.* Employees discuss how their team's goals further the business strategy

and teamwork of the organization. Executives indicate how they see the team's role in the company and discuss with employees their common direction.

2. *Allocate resources.* The company backs up its talk with a budget and assigning people to the team to complete its mission.

3. *Include skilled, relevant people.* People who are specialists in technical areas, in facilitating groups, and in linking with management will all help the team accomplish its goals. Team members discuss their previous accomplishments, experiences, and credentials, and in other ways they realistically disclose their personal strengths.

4. *Develop abilities.* Team members take courses, read books and journals, and discuss ideas so they can keep current in their specialities. Readings, workshops, and reflection on experiences develop skills in dealing with conflicts and other group issues.

5. *Structure opportunities to work together.* Regular meetings, having offices close together, electronic mail, and computer systems help team members exchange information and keep each other posted.

6. *Commit publicly.* The team members indicate they are personally motivated to get the group's job done well. Their public announcement convinces them and others that the team will apply its collective abilities to get the job done.

7. *Hold individuals accountable.* Each team member reports on his or her activities to the group and shows his or her personal responsibility. Individuals who complete their assignments are recognized. The team confronts individuals who fail to fulfill their obligations and may decide to encourage and give assistance or to reprimand and punish the individual.

8. *Structure team human resource systems.* The organization rewards group effort, uses teamwork as a criterion for promotion, provides training in group skills, and makes consultation on teamwork available.

9. *Allow teams to make mistakes.* If management second-guesses team decisions and allows them little autonomy to

experiment with new ways of working together, the team will not accept responsibility for its actions or feel empowered to effect change.

Explore: How to Make Decisions?

Since the general or prevailing opinion on any subject is rarely or never the whole truth, it is only by the collision of adverse opinion that the remainder of the truth has any chance of being supplied.

—*John Stuart Mill*

There never were in this world two opinions alike, no more than two hairs or two grains: the most universal quality is diversity.

—*Michael E. deMontaigne*

Working together and feeling empowered do not mean smooth sailing and inevitable success. Teams hit bumps and bruises along the way. Every group needs the ability to identify and dig into issues and to overcome barriers to move toward its vision.

Issues and decisions come in such a great variety that there is no one particular way that they should be approached. The first rule is that the team must be flexible and use the approach appropriate to the situation. "If the only tool you have is a hammer, you will treat everything as a nail." A leader or coordinator can dispense with minor issues efficiently. Some decisions are not worth the effort to explore in great depth, and previous solutions can be reasonably applied. At times, some decisions must be made quickly with little or no consultation.

What is critical is how the team approaches important, ongoing issues, for these are the decisions that give the group its character and impact on people's involvement and team success. For these issues, the team should dig into issues, create alternatives, and chose a high-quality solution that solves the problems and strengthens the group. The second rule of decision making is that teams need to promote constructive controversy to explore issues and alternatives.

Controversy involves differences of opinion that temporarily prevent, delay, or interfere with reaching a decision. Controversy, when constructively handled, very much contributes to successful teamwork. Through controversy, people become open to new and opposing information. Confrontation with an opposing view creates doubts that one's own position is adequate. People become interested in the arguments of opponents and ask questions to explore them. They take the information seriously, develop a more complex and accurate view of the problem, and incorporate the opposing positions into their own thinking and decisions. Controversy creates new solutions by integrating previously assumed, unrelated, or opposing information and ideas. People appreciate the issues more completely and are committed to implementing solutions because they understand the rationale and purpose.

To be successful the controversy must reaffirm the team's unity and empowerment. Controversy discussed in a win-lose, competitive, "I'm right, you're wrong" way or that questions people's abilities and motives tears teams apart and creates closed-mindedness and one-sided, ineffective solutions. Treated well, controversy will increase the trust and unity of the group.

Teams explore issues thoroughly by protecting and stimulating diverse views. They search for opposing ideas and integrate them to create workable solutions. Strategies to encourage exploring are:

1. *Include diverse people.* Independent people who differ in background, expertise, opinions, outlook, and organization function are likely to disagree.
2. *Establish openness norms.* Everyone is encouraged to express his or her opinions, doubts, uncertainties, and hunches. Ideas are not dismissed because they first appear too unusual, impractical, or undeveloped.
3. *Protect rights.* The rights to dissent and free speech reduce fears of retribution for speaking out.
4. *Assign opposing views.* Coalitions are formed and given opposing positions to present and defend. One person is assigned to take a critical evaluation role by attacking the group's current preference.
5. *Probe.* Team members stop defending their own views long enough to ask each other for more information and

arguments. They put themselves in each other's shoes by listening carefully and reflecting back on the other's position and arguments.

6. *Use the golden rule of controversy.* Discuss issues with others as you would want them to discuss issues with you. If you want people to listen to you, then listen to them.

7. *Consult relevant sources.* Articles, books, consultants, and experts can provide experiences and ideas that can help the group decide which course of action is superior.

8. *Emphasize common ground.* Throughout the discussion, they remind each other that they are working for a solution that benefits all. Team members recognize that they want to resolve the controversy so they can make a decision and accomplish common goals.

9. *Show personal regard.* They criticize ideas rather than attack an individual's motivation and personality. Insults or implications that challenge another's integrity, intelligence, and motives are avoided.

10. *Combine ideas.* Team members avoid "either my way or your way" thinking and try to use as many ideas to create new, useful solutions. They may be able to create a totally new solution.

Reflect: How Can We Improve?

Habits can't be thrown out the upstairs window. They have to be coaxed down the stairs one step at a time.

—Mark Twain

Groups have a choice: they can become more committed to their visions, more united, more empowered, and more capable of exploring issues, or they can undermine their purpose and confidence. Teams need to be able to assess their present state of functioning, to celebrate and build upon their accomplishments, to learn from mistakes, and to deal with frustrations. Effective groups monitor and regulate themselves so that they can continue to work together without a great deal of intervention by managers. They build themselves up into an independent team that will be productive in the future as well as the present.

The status quo has the illusion of permanence. Kurt Lewin argued that the present state of affairs is created by the equilibrium of forces that are presently in balance. Yet these forces will inevitably change and push groups to a new plateau. There are, for example, forces that help team members feel united, but also ones that push them apart. Their present sense of unity results from the balance of these forces. But if a fight convinces people they cannot work together, they feel less confident and united. Groups are either growing or declining. Maintaining the status quo is seldom a real alternative.

An essential first step is to create valid, useful information about the group's present functioning.[4] Organization development specialists have created a rich array of methods to collect data. Team members complete a survey questionnaire and later receive a summary of the results. Process consultation focuses on observing group functioning and then discussing these findings with the group to help them become more aware and effective. Interviewing identifies the perspectives and experiences of group members. Group members as well as outside consultants use these methods to assess the present dynamics of the team.

The data should be useful; it should focus on areas that the group can influence. The team organization model identifies envisioning, uniting, empowering, and exploring as areas to assess and develop.

Avoiding and smoothing over frustrations and conflicts are seldom effective strategies. Indeed, dealing openly and directly with conflict is critical for groups to maintain and strengthen themselves. Through conflict people become aware of frustrations and where their vision, unity, empowering, and exploring are deficient. Conflict creates the incentives and energy to deal with problems. Well-managed conflict is the medium for updating and developing teams.

The team assesses its strengths and successes as well as its frustrations and limitations. Celebrating "small wins" encourages the team to build upon its abilities to accomplish its long-term vision. The team recognizes that it must go through the envision, unite, empower, explore, and reflect cycle continually. An effective team does not appear quickly or easily; team members must think in terms of continuous improvement and ongoing development, not a one-step, quick fix.

The methods teams can use to analyze their interaction, to deal with frustrations, and to celebrate their successes include:

1. *Collect data.* Questionnaires are a relatively inexpensive means for team members to indicate how they view the group's vision, unity, empowerment, exploring, and reflection. In interviews, people explain the specific behaviors and incidents that lie behind their perceptions and generalizations about the group. A team member, an employee from another group, or a consultant can observe the actual interactions within the group.

2. *Structure times to discuss findings.* Team members avoid surprises that catch people off guard and instead have regular, scheduled times to discuss their relationships.

3. *Put self in other's shoes.* Team members ask about and try to know each other's perspective so they can appreciate problems fully and be in position to develop solutions that work for all. They stop defending their own views long enough to listen carefully to others and demonstrate their understanding of the other's position and arguments.

4. *Define issues specifically.* Teams can resolve concrete conflicts more easily than general principles and grand ideas. People fight over issues, not personalities. People talk about their feelings and reactions to the team and its members and describe what has led them to draw their conclusions.

5. *Use exploring and controversy skills.* Team members invite various possibilities, avoid assuming that the solution has to be one person's way or another's, and combine ideas.

6. *Recognize the gains of resolving conflicts and the costs of not doing so.* It takes a team to get itself into a fight, and it takes the team to get out of it. When everyone realizes the costs and the benefits, discussion is apt to be fruitful.

7. *Be firm, yet flexible.* Team members should be firm in their resolve to develop useful solutions, but flexible about what those solutions might be.

8. *Strive for ongoing improvement.* Teams need time to

develop, and interpersonal problems are not easily solved. The goal is to make progress through repeated discussions rather than to solve all issues and become a completely successful team instantly.

The team organization model identifies hurdles a collection of individuals must overcome to be a high-performance team. Teams require a lot. Members must be committed to the team's vision and task, feel united in their purposes, feel empowered that they can do it, be able to explore opposing views, and reflect on their experiences to strengthen their vision, unity, empowerment, and exploring. But these teams give a lot. They drive organizational innovation and continuous improvement and provide a rich, human experience that binds people together and to their organization.

PART TWO

Establishing the Team Organization Framework

Leaders call upon people to take up the challenge to create and pursue the organization's vision. They initiate action to form the teamwork necessary for high performance and high commitment. Yet they cannot create the organization alone. The question is not whether employees should be involved in developing the team organization but how, because creating teamwork requires the head, heart, and feet of managers and employees.

The team organization model provides an ideal to aspire to and a guide to how to proceed. Together managers and employees consider teamwork so that they have a comprehensive understanding and develop a united conviction to become a team organization. They empower each other by providing resources and procedures to work together, explore problems to create ways to collaborate, and reflect on their progress to continue to strengthen their organization.

Teamwork is not a product to buy and lay on a company. It is through people sharing their knowledge and hopes, confronting their differences and dealing with ambiguities that they become committed to teamwork and understand what they must do to be successful. Chapter 5 examines how the management team learns about team organization and begins to model the way. In chapter 6 middle managers find ways to become committed to team organization. Because many employees form teams but often to protect themselves from management, chapter 7 shows how Brian and the management group approach unions to develop team industrial relations. Chapter 8 sketches how a department can be transformed into a team in which people seek out ways to assist and support each other as they pursue company goals.

5

Storming and Forming the Management Team

The five separate fingers are five independent units. Close them and a fist multiplies strength. This is organization.

—J.C. Penney

Where there is much desire to learn, there of necessity will be much arguing, much writing, many opinions; for opinion in good men is but knowledge in the making.

—John Milton, Doctrine and Discipline

Lance and Calvin, though not firm allies and often on opposite sides, on occasion turned to each other. They could not necessarily articulate when this would happen, and both recognized the limits of their mutual confidence. They did know that they could talk to each other at times when they could not talk with Anthony or Janine. They had, for example, quietly comforted each other when Brian was promoted over them.

"Are you ready to be a team?" Lance asked.

"First he gets promoted before us, and now we have to put up with his 'I got to make a difference' campaign," Calvin said.

Lance and Calvin recognized that they weren't highly antagonistic to Brian—they found him a decent fellow—and that a campaign against their boss would be political suicide. Yet they were unprepared to tie themselves and their careers to Brian.

"I can just see the troops in revolt," Lance said. "First they will expect too much, and when little happens, they will be even more demoralized. Talking without follow-up is asking for trouble."

"I can't see this team thing anyway," Calvin said. "Tell me one great thing ever done by a committee."

Lance and Calvin found their talk ventilating and satisfying, but it was not a meeting of the minds. Lance doubted they would implement the program; Calvin questioned the idea of teamwork. They steered away from their differences in favor of emphasizing their common skepticism of Brian's team organization idea.

Excited about the possibilities of PMG's becoming a team organization, Brian was still unsure that his managers were committed. They were trying to understand, but he doubted whether they really believed. Even if the team organization model captured their heads, it would still need to capture their hearts. Without their support, he'd have to scale back his plans or face disrupting the division.

Then it hit him: let the managers debate the model. They can voice their reservations and have their problems addressed. Controversial discussion would underline that the team organization does not insist on harmony but values diversity and disagreement. Brian had encountered the idea that controversy develops understanding and builds commitment in his executive development program. He remembered how counterintuitive the idea seemed at first, but how sensible it seemed now.

"We have been talking and reading about team organization for a week now," Brian began a meeting with his managers. "It occurs to me that you guys might assume that you have to agree with the model. That is not so. If we are going to succeed, you must believe in the idea. I don't want to force you."

"Coercion and working as a team wouldn't seem to go together," Lance said with a laugh. Brian's introduction had gotten his adrenalin flowing.

"Agreed," Brian answered. "Plus the team organization is not the end of knowledge. The model needs to be improved and must be altered to fit our circumstances. I want us to think about our reservations about team organization, especially as it applies to PMG, and form pairs—Anthony and Lance form one, Calvin and Janine another—to talk about them. In fifteen minutes we can get together for a general discussion. Okay?"

The managers agreed with Brian's logic, but they felt unsure and nervous. Lance and Calvin looked around the room, and Janine smiled at Brian. Then Anthony laughed to himself and began to jot down some notes, and that helped the others get going. Soon Anthony and Lance began to talk and Calvin and Janine followed. In a few minutes the room was filled with talk.

"I wish we had as lively a discussion when we were trying to understand the model as when we're criticizing it," Brian teased. "Let's hear first from Calvin and Janine."

"One of the problems we had," Calvin began, "is that we are not sure that teamwork can deliver. We don't want a lot of people just relying on each other and feeling good about each other; there's a lot of tough work to be done. I think the heart of the issue is whether it will help our people lease space, maintain property, clean the halls, and the many other things we need to get done."

"Another problem we had in our group was whether we managers could really show our people what teamwork is," Janine said. "If we do not ourselves cooperate effectively, we will not only look like hypocrites ourselves but our people will take our actions more seriously than our words."

"In our group we were concerned that people have already had too many new programs thrown at them, and then apparently discarded," Lance said. "We can't afford to do that again, and we are unsure that we have a plan to follow through."

"The other issue we talked about is in some sense the opposite," Anthony said. "To me the idea that we need to work as a team is so obvious that I am tempted to assume that everyone else sees it as well. But obviously they do not. So we have work to do and conflicts to manage."

Looking at his notes, Brian summarized and wrote on the board, "We have four important issues to consider: What is the evidence that teamwork can help us be productive and effective? Are we prepared to work as a team ourselves? Do we have the knowledge and persistence to see it through? And are we willing to deal with the reality that not everyone is going to agree with the team organization idea?"

They began by debating the evidence for teamwork because if they could not believe it was useful then issues of implementing it become superfluous. They went back and forth with a mix of seriousness and playfulness. At first they formulated and argued their positions, rephrased, and reargued them. But then they began to listen to each other, ask questions, and reexamine the arguments and evidence in their articles and books.

After forty-five minutes that seemed to them like ten, Brian interjected, "This is fun; a debate a day keeps boredom away!"

"Every other day, please," Janine said with mock pain.

"I think this kind of discussion is great, especially when everyone ends up agreeing with me," Calvin said to a chorus of groans.

"Seriously, it is easy to see Calvin's point, but then I think it is easier to argue against a new way of working rather than develop a new way. 'Better the devil we know than the devil we don't know,'" Janine said.

"We need to wind up our discussion for today." Brian said. "We have not decided much, but some things are clear. We should go back and look at the logic and evidence behind team organization. As I've said before, we must understand and be convinced ourselves before we can expect others to follow. If we are going ahead, we must have a plan to approach and involve the other managers and employees."

"But we have made progress in one area of concern," Lance said. "We demonstrated today that we can work as a team in which people say what is on their mind, listen to each other, and then try to put the best ideas together."

"So we *can* do it," Janine said. "But that means that we must continue to do so, and we need to demonstrate that to our supervisors and employees."

"That's a challenge," Calvin said. "It really asks us to work in a new way. I don't think one or two good discussions are enough."

"Can I suggest that we get away from the office for a day or two to look at ourselves?" Janine inquired. "The team organization helps us define the ideal we want to strive for, but we need a close look at the reality and what we can do to close the gap between what we want and what we are."

"I don't like the idea of retreats," Lance said. "But if we're going to be serious about this, then we probably need one. It would certainly show our people that we are committed and want to follow through."

"What I think is important is not projecting an image of a well-oiled, 'got it all together' team, but instead working toward becoming a successful team that is willing to face our shortcomings and conflicts," Brian said. "The retreat would help to show that."

"Let's find a way to remove the pressure for all of us at PMG to be perfect team players," Anthony said.

"That's where the reflect part of the model comes in," Janine said. "We're committed to examining how we work together and attempting to improve the team, but we don't have to pretend to be perfect."

"We may need an outside facilitator to help us do this," Anthony said. "Someone trained in getting feedback and helping us use it."

"How about a referee . . . someone who can push apart heavy weight boxers," Calvin suggested.

"We need a lion tamer," Lance said to more laughter.

"If I can be serious for a moment, the outside person could help us better understand teamwork and the research behind it," Anthony said.

"Let's look into a day or two away from the office and maybe someone to help us," Brian said.

"I was thinking that our discussion today helps identify how we can approach our people," Anthony said. "Somehow we want them to work to understand team organization, debate its pros and cons, and think about how they can model it for employees."

"But how do we do that with a room full of people?" Calvin asked "It is one thing for five of us to discuss it, but another for forty-five?"

"Anthony's right," Lance said. "I don't think you can just give a pep talk and expect to have them work as a team."

"I'm not so sure I'm good at pep talks anyway," Brian said soberly.

"Brian, we can do it," Anthony said.

"That's right," Janine said. "There's five of us and certainly we can come up with a plan."

"The team organization model should help us make a plan," Calvin said.

"It's supposed to be both the ends and the means," Anthony said. "If we want the team organization, the way to get there is the team organization. We need people to get committed to the vision of a team organization, united behind it, feeling empowered, exploring and reflecting."

"We could use our retreat to think about how we can do that with our managers," Lance said.

"One other thing, one other challenge," Calvin said. "About Charles, if he's not on our side, we might be left twisting in the wind."

"Good point," Brian said. "People must see that he is supporting us. I don't want to surprise him, and I've begun initial discussions to let him get used to the idea. He seems open enough to the idea; teamwork is a part of those management books about quality and serving the customer he's been reading. My promise to you is to keep managing that relationship. I'm not going to ask people to go ahead if the boss will hold it against them."

"That needs to be known," Calvin said.

"I can sense we have more unity behind the team organization idea," Brian said. "But we don't want to close off discussion and debate. We will need all of our effort and good will to become a team organization."

Using Resistance to Build Commitment

Teamwork requires intellectual understanding, emotional conviction, and authentic action. Instead of selling and cajoling, Brian took the opposite track of encouraging the managers to voice their ideas and letting them be heard. Brian was most persuasive when he showed a willingness to listen and take others' ideas seriously.

Teamwork must be forged and created, not decreed from on high. The executive's vision of a team organization is but a first step. Managers, supervisors, and workers must understand the nature of teamwork, be convinced that it is reasonable and useful, feel inspired to pursue it, and have the confidence that they can do it. For this kind of commitment, people need to struggle with and dig into the ideas, voice their concerns, and create a way to foster teamwork that fits them and their circumstances.

Confronting Ambiguities

Calvin was skeptical that teamwork would be productive, Lance doubted they could implement it, and Janine wondered if the managers could be a ideal team. Brian recognized that these uncertainties could be put to productive use if they were discussed openly and constructively.

After doubts are expressed in controversy, people recognize the information and ideas needed to address each other's concerns. They counter each other's arguments and ask each other questions. They check errors of logic and omissions of fact.

In addition to improving reasoning, controversial discussions are emotionally rewarding. People feel relieved that they can speak their hesitancies and concerns candidly and do not have to expend the energy and time to pretend they are in agreement. Active discussion helps people believe they have been dealt with fairly, even when they do not get what they want. But for controversy to have such salubrious effects, people must discuss their differences as a cooperative team.

Changing Attitudes

People must emotionally believe as well as intellectually understand teamwork. Reading and discussing help build commitment; it is hard to be committed to something that you don't understand.

Yet reading, talking, and understanding are insufficient. Attitudes toward cooperation and competitive are deeply held and based on people's beliefs about themselves, human nature, and the reality of organizations. People continually act on these attitudes and have developed their own rationales and defenses for their behavior based on cooperation and competition. A tough, controlling boss is not going to admit quickly that his assumption that he must be competitive to be effective is wrong and that the troubled relationships he has created for twenty years have been counterproductive!

People need time to reflect, consider, and experiment with the idea of cooperative teamwork if they are to embrace its value. Perhaps the most convincing evidence is personal involvement in productive teams. Through reflection, people experience and understand very concretely the emotional and "bottom-line" benefits of this idea. Remember, people do not have to relinquish their idea of the value of competition, but only to understand that its uses are much more limited than commonly assumed.

Becoming Authentic

Even with their heads and hearts on their side, Brian and his managers must act as a cooperative team. Then the message of team organization becomes credible; then the management team models the way for the rest of the organization. Brian and his managers must confront their frustrations, turf protection tactics, and interpersonal aloofness and create more effective ways of working together.

The good news is that the team organization does not require perfection. Teamwork is too complex, demanding, and changeable for that. Instead the ideal is that team members are making an honest attempt to work as a team, to reflect on their actions, to receive feedback, and to make a renewed effort to succeed. Trust is based not on the expectation that it will never be violated, but on there being an honest attempt to support and a willingness to discuss conflicts. Authenticity is based on commitment and follow-through as the team moves toward the team organization ideal.

Constructive controversy is a way of making use of resistance to the team organization. To be constructive, people must open-mindedly consider each other's views, work for mutual and win-win solutions, and integrate views effectively. Through such discussion as well as the experience of working as a team, people clarify their ambiguities, become more accepting of cooperation, and begin to implement the model. They demonstrate clearly that disagreement and conflict are part of working successfully as a team.

The Team Organization Model: Means and Ends

The team organization model summarizes both what is to be attained and how to attain it. It describes the ideal of teamwork and indicates the kind of teamwork necessary to get there. Brian, his managers, and their employees must envision a team organization that they understand and believe in, feel united behind it, empower each other to act as a team, explore difficulties and create a plan to become a team organization, and must reflect on their progress and take action to move toward their vision of a team organization.

As Janine argued, team organization requires planning and implementation, whereas the status quo requires no explicit action and change. The team organization model describes the general characteristics and processes of successful teams; it does not identify concrete actions that you should take to make your team constructive. The model also provides the framework for how to work with the whole organization. But here, too, the model provides a guide and people must work together and debate to develop a plan.

You may argue teamwork cannot happen in your company because there is no history of people working together and few common projects. People mind their own business and have their own tasks to do; consequently, there is nothing to get them to work as a team. But becoming a team organization is a common task that requires everybody's participation. The way to become a team organization is through creative, cooperative teamwork. The method reinforces the message. As people work together, they search for ways to combine their ideas, resources, and energy to further their mission and strengthen their team organization.

6

Involving Middle Managers
and Supervisors

If you want one year of prosperity, grow grain.
If you want ten years of prosperity, grow trees.
If you want one hundred years of prosperity, grow people.
                                    —*Chinese proverb*

The honor of one is the honor of all
The hurt of one is the hurt of all.
                                    —*Creek Indian Creed*

"I'm having fun," Brian said to Martin on the phone. He described how the management team had gotten away for a day to look at themselves. The day had not been without its tense moments as they each talked about the strengths and the frustrations they saw in the team and its individual members. The facilitator had them listen to each other's accomplishments and cheer each other on, and that seemed strange, too. "The overall effect was that we *feel* more like a team," Brian told Martin.

"I hope you can keep the good feelings going," Martin said.

"We need action, too," Brian said. "I think we began to deal with an issue that has been bothering a couple of managers. Calvin teased me about how young I was to be promoted, but his voice showed he wasn't really laughing. I exercised discipline. I didn't get huffy and raise my eyebrows, but I didn't let it slide either. I asked him to tell me if he was upset about my promotion. He was embarrassed, but I tried to reassure him that he had no reason for apologizing or being ashamed. Wanting to be promoted after so many years of effective service to the company was a natural feeling. But we shouldn't let it get in our way. I told him that I want him to succeed as much as possible, and that I hope he wants me to succeed as well."

"Sounds good, sounds powerful."

"It had drama. One incident does not make a relationship, but I think it was symbolically and practically an important step."

"That's just great, Brian. I'm delighted. Should I buy you lunch for your work or should you buy me lunch because of your progress?"

They had momentum, Brian and the managers realized, but they needed to keep it going. The daylong meeting with the forty-six middle managers and supervisors they had scheduled for next month would be critical. Brian had already had the first management meeting on the division's business vision: to gain stature within the company by contributing significantly to its profit performance through creative leasing, aggressive marketing, and preventive maintenance programs. Instead of concentrating on developing the leadership and teamwork they needed to achieve their vision, they assumed they already had what they needed.

Brian and his managers brainstormed on how they could best use the next daylong meeting. They agreed that the focus should be on the team organization vision for PMG as the means to achieve its business goals. It was also agreed, most slowly by Brian, that he should begin by talking about his own vision of the division becoming a team organization. Brian protested that he was not the inspiring type, but they reassured him there was no need for a two-hour tearjerker, only a sincere statement in his own words about why he wanted a team organization and why it was good for people and for the company. He should let the middle managers know that they are at the very heart of the division for they create the teamwork necessary for success.

But Brian's talk was only a beginning. How could they get everyone involved so that they would discuss and debate, much as the management team had earlier? They thought that opening up the issues for general discussion would be ineffective because only a few people would talk and the discussion would be disorganized. The idea that such a discussion was their only option was disheartening.

Then Brian remembered that one of his professors had taught strategies to involve a large class of students in a discussion. Brian and Janine would meet with the professor for suggestions how to organize and design the session.

The management team wanted the participants prepared for the meeting. They briefed them on the topic and agenda and made articles and books available. The middle managers thought teamwork and leadership sounded good but were not altogether clear about what would be happening. When the day arrived, most were both hopeful and uncertain.

Brian's talk was well received. He did not pretend to be an impressive, entertaining orator, but he was credible. He told them that for the division to accomplish its business mission, the middle managers must make it happen; if he and the management team were to succeed, middle managers must succeed. "I neither want to nor can be successful without you; only when all of us work together can any of us fully succeed," he stressed. "The emphasis has to be on our mutual effectiveness and success." The challenge of middle managers would be to collaborate with each other and with employees who do the work and serve the customer.

But teamwork is even more important than company success. "Feeling part of a larger vision, working together shoulder-to-shoulder, eye-to-eye, cheering each other on make us very human and humane. I want us to be proud of our company because we care about each other."

"Working as a team has big payoffs for the company and for us as people. But to realize our common vision, we must actually practice teamwork. Today begins the sharpening and refining of our skills, sensitivities, and procedures to work and live together."

Few managers could resist the pull of Brian's talk, and several were noticeably moved. Yet it was only a speech.

After a break, Brian used the team organization model to describe the kind of teamwork he and the management team were striving to realize. First they would try to understand the model in depth, then they would criticize it and discuss how it might apply to them.

Janine used an overhead projector to help describe how they would learn more about the model. First they would form five groups, and each group would be assigned to one aspect of the team organization model. Each person within the group should become enough of an expert on the assigned part that he or she could teach others. Then new groups would be formed comprising one person from each of the original five groups. The goal was for everyone to become an expert in one area and knowledgeable about all five components of team organization and how they are related. Then everyone would be in a better position to criticize the model and understand its implications.

Janine calmly answered questions about the procedures and reassured them that she would be giving instructions as they proceeded. She explained that she wanted the groups to have a mix of people who didn't normally work together so that they could get better acquainted. She read off the overhead the names of people in the five groups and gave each group an overview of one of the team organization model components, which were described in chapter 4.

Within each group, people read the overview and asked and answered each other's questions. In twenty minutes they were ready to move on to the next phase. Janine organized them into seven new groups containing at least one person from each of the original five groups. They took twenty-five minutes to teach each other the five parts and discuss how the components reinforce one another.

After this discussion, Anthony reminded them that the team organization model is not perfect and asked them to consider its limitations and weaknesses. Fifteen minutes later, the groups reported that the model was general and did not specify procedures or how to become a team. Some argued that the model was too idealistic; others that the model was too abstract for their workers to follow.

Lance proposed that these limitations could also be looked on as challenges. The management team was trying to wrestle with limitations; this meeting was an attempt to find a way to put the model into concrete practice.

After lunch, five new groups were formed and each was asked to identify how PMG could put one aspect of the team model into practice. They were to suggest both steps that could be done immediately and long-term changes that would require ongoing work.

After an hour of intense work, the groups reported back a number of sensible suggestions and a few unusual ones. The envision group came up with a possible team symbol for PMG and recommended that all new recruits to the division receive literature about team organizations. The "unite" group argued that the division needed some kind of profit sharing or gain sharing as a tangible sign that people need to work together to succeed; they thought that the compensation needed to be reviewed thoroughly to make it more fair and unifying.

The empower group suggested regularly scheduled, daylong management sessions and that at least part of the time should be devoted to leadership and teamwork issues. The group also wanted training programs on team leadership. The group discussing "explore" proposed that the division explicitly support the right of dissent, but this right had to be exercised responsibly. How to put this right and responsibility into practice would require planning. The "reflect" group wanted to formulate a time line for becoming a team organization and then use regularly scheduled sessions to evaluate progress and keep things moving.

"If I could ask something here," Ricardo interjected. "What I do not understand is how we're supposed to explore issues together. It's not practical for all of us to sit around one table."

"And we have too many problems anyway," Lu said to laughter.

"We agree we don't want everyone in on every issue," Anthony said. "We're thinking of asking people from various parts of the organization to form a task force on high-priority issues that need lots of exploration and discussion."

"Who would be on it?" Moto asked.

"Good question," Anthony responded. "I'm not sure we have the answer."

"I presume we might invite some people and also ask for volunteers," Calvin said.

"The idea, I think, is to get a mix of people so that the task force would really represent the company," Brian said.

"Would that include union people?" Moto asked.

"Another good question, but I don't see why they shouldn't be included, especially on issues that affect them," Brian said. "They would have to be included when we discuss problems related to the collective agreement."

"I think so, and I was hoping you would, too," Moto said.

"How come we're not meeting with the union people?" Lois asked. "We have to start talking to them as well. We're the ones that have to live with management-labor competition."

"I'm glad you're thinking ahead," Brian said. "We do need to talk, and we're talking to union people, but we have to do things slowly and in the right order. Part of it depends upon the people above us at Merchant setting the proper tone with the union. They want to, but it might take them time to do it."

"Tell them to fast-track it," Jake said sharply. "Fighting between management and unions may seem abstract to you at the top, but we are the ones who have to put out all the brush fires."

"Wait until I approach my people about teamwork and working together, they're going to think I've been on the moon," Ricardo said. "I can hear them crying already, 'You exploit us all year long, and now you want us to be happy about it.' There's an awful lot of 'poor me' anger in the workforce."

"Yes," Marilyn added. "And we're supposed to be stoic flak catchers protecting top management from putting up with worker anger."

Brian acknowledged, "I can see that when we don't get our act together at the top of the organization, you in the middle have to pick up the pieces. It is something that we want to change. To me, if we're together as a management group, then we're in a much better position to reach out to the union in a credible, disciplined way."

"I'd like to get back to the issue of task forces—who decides what to do with their recommendations? All of us?" Marilyn asked.

"Yes, in a way," Brian said. "In general, how I see it happening is the task force or perhaps the management team would make a proposal for how to attack a certain problem, like a compensation program that would be more fair and unifying, and then we would debate it. For example, we could form groups of three, and these groups would discuss the recommendation. If they disagree with it, they would suggest what might be done to improve the solution. With effort, we all, or at least most of us, can believe that the final solution is the best we can do."

"So if we're not on the task force, we can still get our crack at the issue in one of these meetings," Ricardo said.

"That's how I see it," Brian replied.

"On the one hand it's good that people can put in their two cents worth, but what about the task force members?" Lu asked. "They have done their best, and then they must be exposed to all sorts of potshots."

"I suppose so," Brian said with puzzlement.

"That won't happen . . . we're all responsible," Anthony said, trying to protect Brian.

"I can see the sparks flying already," Jake said. He was a fifteen-year veteran of PMG and had gotten a reputation among top management as a troublemaker. The truth was he liked the give-and-take of a fight.

"We are not *all* cantankerous types," Anthony trying to deflect the conflict with humor. He did get a few laughs, but he irritated and embarrassed Jake.

Several people went to Jake's defense by arguing that they, too, saw it as a problem. The discussion was becoming more divisive.

Brian knew that he had two problems: how to discuss task force recommendations and the way that Anthony had tried to handle the conflict with Jake. He relaxed as he told himself, "This is still easier than dealing with the conflict with Dereck."

Brian wanted to support both Anthony and Jake as well as to find a solution. "I'm glad you brought up the issue, Jake, and got us thinking about it. We don't have a detailed, error-proof program to lay on you. And our discussions will not always be smooth, but we want to work with you to make our teamwork as successful as possible."

Anthony, still embarrassed, was thankful that Brian had begun to extradite him from a deteriorating conflict. He said, "I want to be open-minded, even though it may not always seem that way!"

"We never offered perfection," Lance said.

"It's okay," Jake said, "I'm not perfect either."

The mood in the room relaxed as Lois teased, "That's the most startling thing I've learned today."

"I'm still wondering about how we can discuss task force recommendations," Marilyn said.

"Of course we have to take the recommendations seriously," Brian said. "If we didn't, why have a task force? But we don't want to just rubber-stamp them either."

"We should use the task force recommendations to help us come up with the best possible solution," Lance said. "To do that we must debate the recommendations to see their advantages and discover their pitfalls."

"Wait a minute," Jake broke in. "Who is to say that Brian and the management team will accept the recommendations of the task force even after we have modified them?"

"I'm glad you brought that up, Jake," Brian said. "I do not plan to be a rubber-stamp leader. I'm going to have to be convinced that we have a good plan before we go ahead and invest a lot of resources into something. You wouldn't want me to do things that I don't believe in."

"Excuse me, but you have us do things we do not believe in," Jake remarked.

"We're trying to close the gap," Brian responded. "Please do not misunderstand me. I have no intention of having task forces and discussions and then just doing it the way I originally planned. That would be dishonest and wasteful. Nor does everything have to have my okay; that would be a bureaucratic mess. But on central issues that hit the whole division, I need to be fully behind the solution. But, of course, I want you all behind it as well."

"I don't want to seem like a rabble-rouser," Jake allowed.

"Remember his name, Brian," came a shout from the back of the room.

"It must warm your heart to have such a supportive team behind you, Jake," Brian said.

"It warms something," Jake said to laughter.

"I think this kind of discussion is just great," Brian said. "I'm learning . . . we're making progress."

"That's it, that's our motto: 'Conflict can be fun,'" Jake said.

"This is fun. Dealing with my teenage son—now that is a tough conflict." Brian's voice softened, "He's a good kid, really, but there are moments . . ."

"Sometimes I think that ever since we gave up the paddle family life has gone downhill," Moto said. "Kids need discipline."

"Families are trying to operate as teams just like we are," Lu added. "I hope we do a better job than many families."

"Teamwork's so vital, but not so easy," Lance said.

"I still have a question about your agreeing to our decisions,"

Jake put in. "Aren't you saying that you must be convinced the solution is the best and that it is less important that we be?"

"Not really," Brian replied. "We don't want to decide these issues on who has more power, but on what is best for all of us and for the whole division. We need to get real consensus behind major programs before we push ahead."

"I think we're getting a better understanding of how we're going to make decisions," Lois said.

"We know better how we can proceed and are not surprised," Lu commented.

"I got another question. Are Brian, Janine, Lance, Anthony, and Calvin the management team, or are we all the management team?" Jake asked.

"My first reaction is that we are all the management team," Janine replied.

"One thing I think will happen is that we will all form smaller management teams within the larger group," Brian said. "These will consist of people we can turn to for information, support, and ideas throughout the week."

"Form a task force to decide our name!" someone from the back shouted.

"Perhaps this is a problem with no solution," Calvin said to more laughter.

Stuck in the Middle

Jake, Marilyn, and others in middle management had an opportunity to vent some of their frustration and anger at the management meeting. There was much more, but they had grown accustomed to protecting themselves from their superiors and approaching them cautiously. They were also skeptical that top management had the determination and the skill to make teamwork really happen. Yet they eagerly put their frustrations and skepticism behind because they wanted to, and they needed to believe.

They felt it was demeaning to be constantly checking up on employees and disciplining them for taking too many trips to the bathroom. They felt suppressed because they knew their bosses did not want to put up with listening to their frustrations. Nor did they have a place to turn to for ongoing assistance. Their peers were busy and did not see it as their role to help, and they avoided talking too candidly with their boss for fear of revealing weaknesses. They had to struggle to make ends meet, and, indeed, they were not much better off financially than the people they managed. Top management might wax on about excellence, but middle managers were in the trenches trying to get by each day.

Teamwork would be an answer, but it also presented a problem. If they were not part of the day-to-day pushing of employees and patching up breakdowns, what would they do? Would they become "redundant" as in many other companies? Or would they become the architects of teamwork? And if they did have to become the architects of teamwork, how would they develop the skills to facilitate teamwork and make PMG what it could become?

The Power of All

Team building has long been an important strategy in developing organizations, but it is typically restricted to groups of five to fifteen. But teamwork is as important, and more difficult, between groups as within them. It is through synergy across divisions and departments that a company develops creative, integrated directions and solutions.

Traditional team building can frustrate such synergy when a team develops a direction at odds with other groups. Team members conclude that although their team is great, the rest of the organization stinks. Other groups protest the group's arrogance, and soon a strong "us against them" climate emerges; groups are too busy fighting each other to serve customers or to worry about the competition.

Brian and the whole management group at PMG, while finding it impractical to have fifty people spend the day talking around one table, benefited a great deal from their day-long meeting. They could sense the power of the whole group's commitment to work together, share a common vision, and feel they were on the same wavelength. They knew they were much more powerful together than separate.

They recognized their limits. They needed a rapport with their employees and union before they could realize their potential. Forging this unity was an important first step to reach out to their employees.

Learning Together: Jigsawing Materials

He who teaches learns twice.

—*Seneca*

To capture the power of all, Brian and his managers had to get on the same wavelength by understanding their teamwork framework. They used jigsawing materials to understand the team organization model and begin to apply it to their division.[1] The steps they used include:

1. Form five groups and give each one the information and materials for one component of the team organization model. Each group should include no more than ten people. If there are more than fifty people in the larger group, then form ten groups with two groups discussing each component.
2. Assign each group the responsibility to become an expert on its part of the model. Each group ensures that everyone in the group understands their part and is prepared to teach that part to people who are learning the model's other components. People share their ideas and develop the best approach possible to teach their assigned component.
3. Learning groups are then formed with one person from each of the five expert groups. Each person in the learning group is responsible to teach his or her part and to learn the other parts of the team organization model. The group discusses how the components complement each other.
4. Groups make presentations and in other ways demonstrate their understanding of the team organization model. They answer questions, identify the model's limitations, and suggest how the organization can use the model.

This jigsawing method can be used to deepen people's understanding of teamwork. For example, people become experts in the elaborate, search, and integrate phases of constructive controversy and then teach each other to understand the 'explore' part of the team organization model.

Jigsawing and other cooperative learning approaches can help managers and employees continually upgrade their abilities and skills. New technology, new markets, and new knowledge require that organizations innovate and managers and employees learn. Literally hundreds of studies, including many field experiments, indicate that cooperative teamwork helps people learn new ideas, develop problem-solving and interpersonal skills, and strengthen their self-confidence.[2]

Brian and the middle managers used cooperative small groups to explore and make suggestions about how PMG could use the model. As they debated these suggestions and made first steps, they would reexamine and refine the model and their thinking. Their understanding would lead to new action which in turn would lead to reflection, deeper appreciation and understanding, and more effective action. In this way, theory informs action and action improves theory.

Ad Hoc Decision-Making Groups

To further their team organization as well as their business, Brian and his managers need to be able to grapple with problems and make decisions. Yet organizations often bungle decision making. People talk in vague generalities, fight over turf, hide information, and nervously protect the status quo. The result is that few options are created, decisions are delayed, the first solution mentioned is adopted, and little is changed. People conclude that they have wasted their time, they doubt the abilities of their colleagues, and they feel like pawns unable to control their destiny.

Participation has long been advocated as a way to steer away from the pitfalls of organizational decision making. Yet inviting employees to help make decisions is not itself enough. The challenge is to involve employees so that there is a lively, constructive discussion of various views and so that they create a responsive solution that deserves their commitment.[3]

But how can this kind of spirited participation be accomplished in large divisions and companies? Representation in task forces, union-management problem-solving teams, and other groups are useful (see chapter 9). Yet even with these small teams larger groups need to consider issues and solutions collectively.

Breaking down a large group into smaller decision-making groups and then re-forming into the larger group is an effective way to foster participation and discussion. People in small groups first debate and explore an issue and form a consensus, and then this process is repeated in the large group.[4]

Ad hoc groups, usually consisting of three persons, can do the following:

1. Listen to a recommendation made by a task force or manager.
2. Decide whether to accept or modify the recommendation and develop a rationale.
3. Present their consensus and rationale to the large group and listen to other reports.
4. Discuss the reports and decide by consensus or majority vote on the final recommendations.
5. Identify the present task force or others to oversee the implementation of the decision.

Brian, the management team, and the middle managers were becoming a team as they discussed their vision of a team organization. To make the method consistent with the message, Brian had to structure active, full involvement of the middle managers so that they could understand the organization vision, express their reservations, and begin to develop the relationships and skills necessary to put a team organization into place.

They were moving, deliberating, and gaining momentum, but they would face additional hurdles. In the next chapter Brian and his managers approach union leaders to confront their win-lose dynamics. In later chapters they will use task forces and other problem-solving teams to deal with important issues as they pursue their objectives and vision.

Reaching Out to Employees and Unions

[After managers and workers] come to see that when they stop pulling against one another, and instead both turn and push shoulder to shoulder in the same direction, the size of the surplus created by their joint efforts is truly astounding. . . . This . . . is the beginning of the great mental revolution which constitutes the first step toward scientific management.

—Frederick W. Taylor

It took employee involvement to bring us together tonight. It took employee involvement to foster a new spirit and attitude that flourished at the bargaining table only seven months ago. And it took employee involvement to chart a new standard for labor and management relations. . . . I believe that we are just beginning to grasp the potential that lies ahead. . . . I want Ford to be recognized by our human enterprise as well as our economic enterprise. . . . We are here because we believe in employee involvement and in mutual commitment to common goals.

—Donald E. Petersen, Ford Motor Company

We are a team. We must treat each other with trust and respect.

—Mission, Values, and Guiding Principles, Ford Motor Company

Getting the managers on the same wavelength gave Brian and his team direction and confidence. It was more satisfying than accomplishing a concrete task; it brought a sense of empowerment that helped toward realizing the potential of a high-performance team organization. They felt invigorated and ready for the next challenges.

Discussions with middle managers made it clear that turning around the management-union relationship was high priority. Brian had hoped his talk with Charles would have been more encouraging. Charles did say the right things about the need to cooperate with the union and gave his official blessing to Brian's working directly with Frank Kincaid, the union leader. But Charles's offhand comments about the union and its leadership were disturbing: "You're going to have to teach Frank the abc's of teamwork," and "Frank is so out of touch with modern developments and with his people. I don't understand why they haven't thrown him out on his ear."

Brian was bothered because Charles's comments reflected the attitudes that had previously undermined labor relations at Merchant. Charles and other managers blamed the messenger. When the union made demands, filed grievances, and on occasion went out on strike, management would angrily denounce the union leadership. They would accuse workers of being short-sighted and unreasonable, but their wrath was directed at the union leadership. They would not change the way they managed; what was necessary was changing union leaders.

Brian sensed, though he had never put it into words, that these attitudes toward union leadership were part of a more general management defense. Merchant had, like other companies of its size, come under increasing pressures from foreign and domestic competition. The recent loss of major projects to new foreign competitors was a blow to Merchant's self-image. Executives consoled themselves that foreign competitors were unfairly advantaged because they did not have to contend with unions.

The union had its own villain: top management. Union leaders portrayed themselves as defending the "little guy" from the power of company executives who, left to their own resources, would find many reasons to keep wages low and hours long. They attributed the failure to land projects to the political infighting and ineffectiveness of top management.

Changing these interwoven, reinforcing attitudes would not be easy. But Brian reassured himself that he did not have to change them single-handedly overnight. Developing a team attitude between management and union would take months but would payoff for years.

"The good news is that Charles is behind our approaching Frank and the union about working together more closely," Brian reported to the management team. "The bad news is that we probably won't get much help."

The managers were not surprised. "I can see the need to change, but I also know that I have some set ideas myself," Calvin said.

Calvin's candor initiated a discussion about how they must exercise discipline to check their obsolete ideas and habits. They would help each other avoid pitfalls and not allow themselves to be swooped up into the old win-lose way of relating to the union.

They favored a gradual approach. Brian would talk one-on-one with Frank and then involve others in the union and management discussion. They would proceed directly to gain momentum, but they would also go slowly enough to give people an opportunity to get involved and change their attitudes.

Frank agreed to a meeting to discuss a "team relationship" and appeared relaxed as the meeting began. Later, Brian would recognize that he wasn't actually as relaxed as it had appeared.

"You talk about a new relationship between management and union at PMG," Frank said. "We're always hopeful about such an occurrence, and we've demonstrated great patience while you guys decide to enter the twentieth century."

Brian could feel himself tense up, but he said to himself, "I don't have to be insulted. I can enjoy his language and his humor."

"Then I guess you won't mind waiting a few minutes longer while I get us some coffee," Brian teased. Frank laughed aloud, and they were off to a good start.

Brian described his vision to become a vigorous and forward-looking division that would contribute substantially to the success of the overall company. He and the managers were trying to move toward the vision of the division as a team organization good for both people and the company.

"All this may sound new to you, but we in the labor movement have known all along that people have to work together," Frank said. "Participative management and teamwork have been part of the union movement for decades. You didn't have to go to executive training for that. Just ask us, and we would have told you."

Brian could have let himself get upset by concluding that Frank was arrogant and rude. He knew it was better to accept Frank as a person who liked to mix it up and speak his mind directly. Perhaps it was Frank's way of letting off steam after years of battling management. Brian reminded himself that he and Frank were largely in agreement in their analysis of what was wrong and what should be done.

"I should have asked you," Brian said. "That would have been easier than going to all those classes."

"And cheaper too." Frank voice softened. "Now I didn't say we could have taught you *how* to create teamwork and participation, but only that you should learn about it."

"Learning how would cost extra?" Brian asked.

"If we knew how, we would have thrown it in at no charge." Frank turned serious. He argued that managing a union was very difficult. "People in management feel obligated to all be on the same side, but in unions everyone has an opinion and everyone has the right to speak out. It makes things interesting, but very tough to manage and keep together. And today union members have seen their counterparts lose their jobs and pensions when businesses go bankrupt and are restructured."

Brian was pleased with Frank's candor. "Perhaps we're not so different that way. We want the kind of team where people speak out and have the right to dissent. We think that our individuality and our differences are real and make life interesting, and that they can be very useful for the company."

"You can express yourselves, but you just don't let us speak up in the union, right?"

Brian saw his opportunity to make a critical point. "No, we want you and the rank and file to be free to speak out, too. We want people to discuss their opposing views, be themselves, and manage their conflicts. That's the kind of team relationship we're talking about, and it certainly allows for a good, strong union."

"You're talking my language. We don't want to be co-opted, to give up our right to protect ourselves and our union just to let you increase profits."

"But the right of dissent carries a corresponding responsibility, which we expect from our managers, and which we hope you can agree to. We're all responsible to develop the kind of team relationship that encourages people to speak out and use their differences productively."

Brian explained that if people use their differences to badger each other, then conflicts won't be very productive for the company and won't help people feel free to speak out. There will be sniping rather than direct discussions.

Frank was interested in these ideas, and he reminded Brian that unions were on the defensive. Unions were losing market share because fewer people were unionized and unions were under the threat of decertification. "It gives us the challenge to be better managers and serve our 'customers.' We are under constant scrutiny both to find new ways of working with management and to protect our people from bad management. Our members can and do vote us out of office. I could be back sweeping the hallways next year. We're more under the gun than managers and we don't have golden parachutes."

Brian and Frank agreed that they should meet with several managers and union officials to get more concrete suggestions about how to begin to develop this relationship. Frank warned Brian that not all the people in the union would see the logic of team organization as clearly as he did, nor would they share his commitment to finding better ways to work with managers. Many union people were angry, and their attitudes would not change overnight.

Brian reported the progress in his discussions with Frank to the management team. He told them that Frank was himself very open and wanted to push forward, but that did not mean others would be. "We must be disciplined and not let ourselves get sidetracked and revert to old ways." Brian described examples of Frank's style that he had almost let push his button. "We can't let differences in style interfere with our common direction and goals." Brian warned that the union people may not always appear cordial.

The management team discussed how to check their outmoded

ideas, exercise self-restraint, and take the long-term view. They reminded themselves not to jump to the conclusion that union leaders are obstructive and committed to the win-lose status quo unless they had hard, irrefutable evidence. They should remain committed to team organization and to creating opportunities to work with union leaders and members.

Brian and Frank were more nervous before meeting with the managers and union leaders than they had been before their own meeting. They recognized that anyone could throw a verbal blow that might ignite an explosion not easily controlled. The union people did not disappoint; they wondered why management hadn't begun this process a decade ago and argued that asking them to trust management was asking a lot. But the management team showed discipline, and the meeting ended with a commitment to forming a joint union-management team that would oversee and develop concrete ways to forge a team relationship. This team might, for example, look at how the collective bargaining process could be improved and how to implement a profit-sharing plan. Management and union did not relinquish authority and would have to approve the group's recommendations.

"Good progress," Brian said in closing the meeting. "I want to discuss this proposal with all the managers, and I assume you want to talk it over with your people," he said to Frank. "If there are only minor changes, Frank and I could get back together and make the final plans."

Brian doubted managers would object, but he wanted to establish the principle of consultation to ensure that middle managers were informed and to solicit ideas about where to go next. At a meeting of all the managers, Brian described the proposal to establish a joint management-union team and then used the ad hoc decision-making groups procedure described in chapter 6 to let them consider the proposal. The managers like the approach, but several groups noted that it was only a beginning and suggested several priorities. There was a general consensus that the joint labor-management task force should consider a division-wide bonus to tie union, management, and the various departments together. These ideas were later forwarded to the management-union team.

Breaking Out of the Win-Lose Union-Management Conflict

Brian and his management team recognized that forging a new relationship with the union would help them create an effective organization that would improve performance and benefit people. They knew the costs of the status quo and wanted change. Yet it was not enough to complain about unions; they had been doing that for years. The management team had to appreciate the costs of the present approach, see a realistic alternative, and find the discipline to create it.

Dealing with the Legacy

Competitive union-management relations at Merchant and other organizations have bottom-line costs. Supervisors and workers spend their time putting out fires and fighting each other rather than getting the job done. Shop floor workers balk at developing new products and implementing new technology instead of becoming allies in innovation and improving services for customers.

Without a firm link with management, employee teams are apt to adopt an antimanagement stance. They coalesce partly around seeing the management as the enemy. Because management is unpredictable and unknown, workers feel they must unite to protect themselves. Workers and managers see themselves as distinct in values and interest: they are not part of the same community, nor do they even share the same humanity. Union and worker solidarity is a countervailing power to the threat of management, and still employees feel uninformed, wary, and unwilling to persist in making vigorous efforts for continuous improvement.

Management and labor, intent on protecting themselves from each other, have failed to develop forums and procedures to iron out difficulties and make decisions constructively. They avoid each other until the problem is so severe that they are forced to meet to resolve the crisis. The threat of a mutually costly strike propels them to search for a stopgap measure to get them by.

The Team Relationship as an Authentic Alternative

In addition to feeling the costs of the present union-management relations, Brian and his managers needed to see a realistic alternative in order to take action. Frank and other union leaders worried that in cooperative programs they would be co-opted and unable to voice their objections and to represent their constituencies. But the team organization does not require such conformity, indeed, it requires the ideas and individuality of union leaders. Managers and workers are committed to open dialogue because they recognize that it is through constructive conflict that problems are identified, solutions are created, and unity is forged.

Traditionally, industrial relations has been viewed from unitarian, Marxist, and mixed-motive perspectives. The unitarian view that the interests of management and workers are one is widely considered too unrealistic as a basis for building a viable industrial relations system.[1] Marxist industrial relations theorists argue that the class conflict over ownership of the means of production causes opposing interests to compete to attain their goals. Management wants to reduce the costs of labor, and workers want to increase its costs. The third, and dominant perspective among industrial relations researchers sees the management-labor relationship as a mixed-motive relationship. The two sides have opposing interests over issues such as wages but overlapping interests on issues such as safety and the financial solvency of the firm. They must negotiate their differences so that they can continue to work on common goals.

The team organization model poses a fourth alternative. It recognizes that management and labor have opposing and common interests but holds that what is critical is how managers and workers consider their interests. They can decide that they have largely competitive interests: management seeks profits and power at the expense of workers. Or they can decide their goals are basically cooperative: they are both committed to company success, employee competence, and job security. Management and labor have the common goal to create a quality relationship that helps them work together to pursue their joint interests.

The conclusion by union and management that their goals are primarily cooperative rather than competitive dramatically affects the dynamics and outcomes of labor relations. Concession bargaining, union representation on boards, profit sharing, quality of work life, and employee involvement programs have been considered signs of a transformation of the U.S. industrial relations system.[2]

Unions' Potential Contribution

Many managers assume that unions make it more difficult, even preclude constructive employee relations. Yet Ford and many companies are finding that union leaders can be partners and allies in developing more constructive labor relations.[3] Union leaders, if convinced that management is sincere, help persuade workers to trust management and experiment with employee involvement. Union leaders can help set up forums and avenues for workers and managers to work together. They remind managers of the need to discuss conflicts and differences openly and constructively.

Workers do not see an inevitable trade-off between company and union. With a cooperative management-union relationship workers can be highly committed to their company as well as to their union.[4] The quality of the relationship between management and workers is critical for employee relations, not whether workers are unionized.

Discipline To Take the First and Subsequent Steps

In the win-lose conflict between management and labor at Merchant, both sides were paying a price and wanted a change. Both had the same solution: since the other side caused the problem, it should take the first step. This mutual conclusion resulted in an agonizing paralysis. But Brian and his management team recognized that they could take the first step.

They realized that could take the next steps, too. They would demonstrate credibility through their determined, consistent effort to establish a new, open, cooperative relationship. The mistrust and habits of years could not be washed away with a few minutes of nice-sounding words and grand gestures.

Brian and his management team did not get distracted or let the boisterous style of the union get in their way. They realized that in a win-lose climate, union leaders and managers are compelled to talk tough to remain credible with their respective constituents. By being disciplined and staying focused on developing the relationship, Brian and his managers gave union leaders concrete evidence that the talk of a lively, team relationship would be followed with consistent action.

Industrial Relations as Competitive Advantage

Many companies are overhauling their industrial relations system. Inflexibility, feather bedding, unearned pay increases, rigid bargaining, and strikes caused jointly by management and labor are no longer acceptable. In the past, managers could avoid these issues and argue that they were not disadvantaged because other companies were having the same troubles. Today many managers realize that effective industrial relations is a critical competitive advantage.

Some managers complacently argued that labor costs and the ineffective management of labor were "taken out of competition" because all firms had the same inefficiencies. Increasingly North American and European companies must compete directly with firms operating with a much different industrial relations system with lower, and sometimes much lower, wage structures. In addition, some of these systems work better because they have improved productivity and cut down on strikes and lost workdays.

Beginning in the 1960s and taking hold in the 1970s, many companies in the United States and elsewhere have deployed an aggressive, successful employee relations strategy, often because they want to prevent unionization.[5] They have developed personnel policies that undercut incentives to unionize: they pay employees well; invest in technology and training of employees; stabilize employment and minimize layoffs; involve employees in making decisions; have developed a rational wage and salary administration and performance appraisal that rewards both merit and seniority; and have selected sites and people who would not be pro-union. IBM, Eastman Kodak, Digital Equipment Corporation, Motorola, du Pont, Michelin Tires, Marriot Hotels, and Sears, Roebuck have found that these strategies promote the company's goals and help avoid unions.

Current research supports these companies' conclusion that cooperative relationships with the workforce contribute to organizational success. Savvy Japanese firms have used information sharing as a strategic industrial relations policy to improve firm performance. Japanese firms that used joint consultation committees were found to be more profitable and productive than those that did not.[6] Information sharing appears to moderate union demands and make them more open to accepting lower wage settlements.[7]

In the United States effective industrial relations programs have contributed to productivity. Organizations with low grievance rates and infrequent disciplinary action were found to have low absenteeism and high participation in suggestion programs; these dynamics, in turn, appear to contribute to labor efficiency and product quality.[8] Concession bargaining can contribute substantially to firm value and shareholder equity, and potentially to future worker gains.[9]

Cooperative relations with workers, whether unionized or not, is a powerful strategy for firms seeking to adjust to market pressures and gain competitive advantages. Quality labor-management relationships and joint consultation are likely to bring about wage concessions when needed and acceptance of employee involvement programs to improve quality and reduce costs. In service industries in particular, consultation with frontline employees enables firms to react faster to changes in the marketplace and to upgrade the quality of service to customers.

Involving Employees for Manufacturing Excellence

The competitive factory of today uses computers, robots, and flexible machines to lower costs, improve quality, and offer greater product variation. The competitive factory of tomorrow will bundle services with products that meet a range of customer needs.[10] Even today production workers are marketing by talking to customers about their needs. They are consulting with customers about how to maintain and use products effectively. The factory has become a showroom for customers to appreciate how the company's products can solve problems.

In mass production the production core has been separated from upstream activities of new product development and design and from downstream activities of sales and service. For decades manufacturing managers have tried to maximize their efficiency and have complained that the demands of new product engineers and salespeople have interfered.

As many Japanese manufacturers have shown, eliminating barriers between the upstream activities of new product and processes and the shop floor fosters innovation and improves manufacturing performance. Getting product designers, manufacturing engineers, and shop floor managers and employees talking and working together are critical for manufacturing excellence. Understanding the aspirations and ideas of new product people and manufacturing engineers, factory managers and workers have become invaluable allies as they provide feedback on the manufacturability of new designs, construct prototypes quickly, and introduce engineering changes.

Tomorrow's Service Factory

Teamwork will be even more critical for the service factory of tomorrow than it has been for the competitive factory of today. In the factory of the future, shop floor managers and workers will be linked with downstream activities to support the sales force, service technicians, and consumers. They will give their companies competitive advantages by serving customers before and after the product has been built as well as manufacturing high-quality, specialized, cost-effective products.

Manufacturers are already experimenting with the service factory. For example, Tektronix, a manufacturer of electronic equipment, has set up a direct communication between customers and shop floor employees. The company inserts a card in every oscilloscope that lists the names of the workers who built it along with a toll-free number. Customers call with questions about the use of their oscilloscopes, complaints about its performance, and requests for additional products. The workers meet daily with managers to discuss the phone calls and necessary follow-up. Workers also call customers and ask how well their products are performing.

At Hewlett-Packard's Fort Collins Systems Division, which makes computers and technical workstations, the factory's quality department supports marketing. The marketing staff is in a position to know what information customers want. The quality department collects and presents information on test results and conditions in easy-to-understand ways, including videotapes, that inform and impress customers. The quality department also works directly with salespeople, using training and guided tours to prepare them to serve customers.

Allen-Bradley, a manufacturer of industrial automation controls, uses its Milwaukee computer-integrated manufacturing operation to demonstrate its products. Within twenty-four hours of the order, the factory can assemble 1,025 different electronic products with zero defects. Customers can see firsthand how various levels of controls work together and how Allen-Bradley's software products and systems architecture can help them be productive.

Teamwork is key to making the full-scale service factory a reality. Factory people must work with marketing and service if they are going to understand customer expectations and become skilled in making presentations, consulting with customers, and opening up their factories as showrooms. Marketing and service people gain essential product information and capabilities by talking with the people who build and know the product the best.

Technology helps with teamwork. Computerized ordering systems, expert systems to manage complex sales, computerized logs for after-sale support, computerized catalogs for replacement parts, and twenty-four–hour answering machines to take customers complaints all speed up communication and break down barriers between production and upstream and downstream activities. However, understanding the value of teamwork and knowing how to work together drive the move to the service factory.

Manufacturing operations continue to require fewer people, but those who remain must do much more than any robot can. They have proven themselves indispensable members of the teams that design and develop new products. They will increasingly become partners with marketing, sales, and after-sales service as their companies strive to meet comprehensive customer needs. The days of functional groups doing their own thing with a few managers trying to coerce some coordination are gone. It is ongoing, face-to-face, spirited teamwork that propels innovation and competitive advantage in manufacturing.

Competitive attitudes between union and management cannot be dislodged and new forums created overnight. Brian and his management team will need to be persistent and credible so that workers and managers can become partners and create the joint oversight committee, problem-solving groups, and other procedures to work together.

Pronouncements about cooperation are insufficient; a team organization is needed to make an industrial relations system authentic. Managers and workers, management and union must together commit themselves to an ongoing effort to develop a cooperative relationship and team industrial relations system.

Management and employee leaders, whether union or nonunion, together need to agree to develop honest, cooperative relations. With joint sponsorship, managers and union leaders do not have to worry that participation makes them appear to be weak or giving in. A central team of industrial relations and other managers and union leaders and workers can stimulate and oversee concrete action.[11]

Teamwork is needed between management, employees, and union up and down the hierarchy to forge a new relationship. Managers tend to assume that workers should "cooperate," and those too "irresponsible" to do so should be terminated. Managers cannot assume but must work persistently to forge cooperative links with workers.

Through strong, cooperative links, managers can work with employees to help them develop teams that foster company productivity and innovation and create working conditions and opportunities that foster employee well-being, competence, and dignity. The next chapter describes how managers and employees can work together to form productive teams.

Forming Employee Teams for Innovation and Commitment

To the extent that we continue to celebrate the traditional myth of the entrepreneurial hero, we will slow the progress of change and adaptation that is essential to our economic success. If we are to compete effectively in today's world, we must begin to celebrate collective entrepreneurship, endeavors in which the whole of the effort is greater than the sum of individual contributions. We need to honor our teams more, our aggressive leaders and maverick geniuses less.

—Robert Reich

The week after the management meeting, Russ Erickson did not seem his usually introspective self at the office. He had spent the weekend mulling over the team organization program Brian appeared intent on pursuing. The team idea stirred him up like he had not been for years.

He thought he had kept his anger to himself. But who could forget all those laughs about accountants as bean counters? Or the defenses of the overblown egos of executives when confronted with poor results: "These numbers are wrong!" He still vividly remembered the management consultants who talked about Merchant being lean and mean and cutting down on overhead. They were not being bold; they were just feeding on prejudices against accountants.

Although he was enticed by its possibilities, the team organization program seemed too radical and challenging to Russ. Reconciled to having little impact on top management and not being on the fast track to the top, he had adapted well to being off the roller coaster of ambition. He and his wife had created a rich life outside of Merchant; they already had plans for his retirement in five years. He still took pride in his job, but it was not an all-consuming interest.

Russ sensed, though no one spoke openly about it, that others in his department had reconciled themselves in a similar way. They relied on the satisfaction of doing their jobs well but never fully committed themselves to the company or each other.

It could not be said that people were inconsiderate and disrespectful. Though there was little socializing outside of work, they were cordial and certainly willing to help one another when asked. Russ remembered how he and others in the department were surprised when a young, capable accounting professional cited the lack of support as his reason for abruptly resigning. They talked about it for a day and then dropped the subject, having come to the common conclusion that he recognized he would have to go elsewhere for quick advancement and power.

Russ's wife enjoyed seeing him enthusiastic as he talked about the team organization workshop. Perhaps he could make one more concerted effort to strengthen the accounting department's role. It would be delightful to retire knowing that the potential of accounting would be realized rather than squandered. He wanted to go out with a bang not a whisper.

Russ worked in the theme of teamwork's contribution to the department as he went about his daily routine. The next week the department met to discuss the team organization program. Russ described the purpose of the managers' workshop and how he was convinced that top management was sincere. He wanted the accounting department to consider such a program for itself.

Russ was surprised that departmental members were so skeptical, though later he realized that what happened was completely predictable. Their skepticism was not so much directed at the purposes and intentions behind the program as at the need for it. There was much talk about how their work relationships inside and outside the accounting department were as good as could be expected. There was, of course, room for improvement, but they did not see a team program as a priority.

Russ challenged these conclusions. He argued that people did not really spend much time discussing common problems. They responded that everyone had their own job, but there had never been a problem getting people to help when help was requested. Russ reminded them that people frequently grumbled about how tough it was to work with many managers outside the department. They responded that such misunderstandings were inevitable because they had to deal with people untrained and uninterested in accounting information.

"Let's face it," Shakeel said. "Managers do not like controls, and it is our role to enforce them. There's always been tension since I've been here and there's always going to be."

"We're seen as the guys bringing bad news," Ruth said. "You don't have to work for Merchant to not like getting bad news."

Russ decided not to push his points at this meeting. Later he and his assistant manager, Angela Salvador, came up with the idea to survey managers to better document how the accounting department was perceived by its "customers," the managers in other units of PMG. After getting a consensus at the next department meeting, Angela arranged with the human resources department to do a survey of how managers perceived the accounting department and what they would ideally want in the accounting department.

Three weeks later, Russ distributed the results and called a meeting to discuss them. The findings were sobering. Managers saw the department as fragmented and disorganized with little common focus and poor coordination. Managers complained they got different messages depending upon which person they talked with, and that one person usually had no idea what others were doing.

What the managers ideally wanted from the department was surprising. They wanted more not less interaction, information, and assistance. They felt accounting data were critical for them as managers, but they were frustrated that the data they got were often too little, too late, and unexplained. They understood the need to justify variances in the budgets, but wanted to find less accusatory ways of discussing them.

As the accounting department reflected on the results, their mood became more upbeat and energetic. Confronting the data together seemed to lift their spirits. It was as if using the data to face reality directly was empowering.

The tough question was what could be done. The mood took on

a more pessimistic flavor as they began to realize that satisfying the managers would take drastic action. There were the usual disclaimers about how they could not improve without adding more resources: "You get what you pay for." People downplayed the need to change: "You can't satisfy everyone."

Russ saw the opportunity to lead and seized it. "I want us to be as good as we can be. The more I have thought about us, the more I realize that we all pay a price for the grumbling about the bean counters in accounting. We are competent professionals, and though we all believe that we deserve to be respected, the fact is that in this organization at this time we are in a hole and must work ourselves out of it. We can wish that managers will change, and perhaps they will, but I think we should take the first steps.

"Now, I'm not saying that I know the answer to how we are going to do this. But I know in my heart that it will take all of us working together, perhaps as we have never done before, to come up with the many answers. I am willing to take the point position, but I need you too."

The accounting group was silenced. They were not accustomed to Russ making empassioned speeches, nor were they comfortable with the explicit expression of feelings. Russ had touched long-standing, touchy grievances but also foreshadowed a way out of their predicament.

"Let's go for it," Ruth broke the silence.

There was growing agreement that they should try to take advantage of the team organization program. Even several of the more skeptical members were saying that they didn't have much to lose.

Russ explained that he thought it best for them to begin working on themselves as a team first. Then as a team they would be better prepared to find ways to strengthen their place in the organization. The next step would be to form a small, representative group that would work with Russ and Angela to develop a program and an agenda that would be considered at the next meeting.

The workshop the department approved at its next meeting was similar to the one the middle managers had chosen. All twelve members of the accounting department met for a day. After Russ restated his conviction about the importance of teamwork for achieving their vision of the department, participants did an exercise illustrating the potential of groups solving problems. People were able to see how combining the information, logic, and ideas of several workers resulted in higher quality solutions than working alone. They also experienced the fun of give-and-take interaction. Through discussion they also realized that team problem solving requires a great deal. People have to speak their minds, listen to each other open-mindedly, combine their information, and integrate their ideas.

To develop a better understanding of the nature of productive teamwork, the group used the jigsaw method (see chapter 6) to learn and teach each other the team organization model. They had lively debates as they questioned and explored the parts of the model and how they reinforce each other.

Five groups were formed, and each one was assigned one part of the model. They were to use their understanding of these parts to make recommendations about how the department could become a team.

Richard served as spokesperson for the "envision" group. "We thought that if we're serious about working together better, we had better change some fundamental ideas we have about ourselves," he began. "We have to see the department as a team rather than a collection of professionals who happen to have neighboring offices. What is perhaps more difficult is that we have to change the way we think of ourselves. Most of us see ourselves as independent people who are strong enough to be self-reliant. Many of us got degrees in accounting so that we would have some tangible, valuable skills and be self-sufficient. That we would have to work together never really crossed our minds. Now we have to see that relating to others is critical to being successful."

"How can we do this?" Shakeel asked. "It all seems so abstract."

"It is," Candice said. "But we've got some specifics, too. We could have social outings together, perhaps have a softball team with Team Accounting written on the t-shirt. We'll try to talk about 'we' and 'us' not just 'I' all the time. These would all help."

Byron gave the "unite" group summary. "What we propose builds right on what the first group discussed. We must recognize that we really do need each other and that others have valuable knowledge and ideas that we need so that we can do our jobs as well as possible. T-shirts and social gatherings would help us feel united. We also thought we should work on our vision, the kind of accounting department we are and what we provide our clients. This would help us think about ourselves as a unit.

"But we wanted to find a very tangible reward that we could earn together. Instead of fretting so much over who gets a 3 percent raise and who gets a 3.5 percent raise, we should find incentives that unite us. They could be a common bonus—though we don't know how we could work that out—or if we do a good job, the boss throws us a Christmas party. It is something we should think about."

"Are you talking about everyone getting the same reward?" Rosalie asked. "Is that practical?"

"It is at least as practical as the boss trying to figure out who deserves a 3.0 percent raise, a 3.1 percent raise . . . as we try to do now," Byron said. "I guess not everyone needs exactly the same reward, but the idea is that we all see that we are all better off the better the group does as a whole."

"That's probably good, but what we really need is an outward bound type rafting trip through the Grand Canyon followed up with scaling canyon walls, then we could survival ski in Utah," Ruth teased.

"Great imagination," Byron said. "Those things can pull people together, though."

"You should see how they push a budget," Russ said with a smile.

After more discussion, Ruth summarized the "empower" group's ideas. "We have to recognize that we have been trained to the nth degree in accounting theory and practice, so we know our stuff. But we have never been trained to communicate, to combine our ideas, and to use all those other people skills. If we're going to feel confident and empowered, we need to work on that.

"Also, we were thinking we need to reorganize. How we think about our jobs, how we get organized, and how we tell others to work with us are all based on the idea that one person does one job. That assumption just permeates our whole operation. But we need to think about how we can assign major tasks to teams."

"But group assignments can be carried too far," Rosalie said. "People loaf and let the other guy do it, and, besides, people take pride in doing their own job."

"We agree," James said. "There's room for people doing a task by themselves. Most things we actually do can probably best be done by an individual. It is just that we all see what we are doing as part of a larger effort, and for major issues and problems we hash things over. And if someone does not do his or her own tasks, the rest of us will have to let him or her know it."

Dawn discussed the "explore" group's findings. "A big barrier that gets in the way of our exploring issues in depth is that we all want to be right. Now, unless by some miracle we all think alike, it is pretty hard for all of us to be right. But we try!"

"But sometimes we don't try at all, and we just let things slide by," Richard said.

"We saw that too," Dawn agreed. "It's like we know that disagreeing will be taken so personally and so hard that we go out of our way to agree with others."

"You mean we pretend to agree with others," Shakeel said. "Once they leave the room, then we show our disagreement. It's gotten so I don't like to leave rooms!"

"Funny, but it's too true to be really funny," Dawn said. She listed advocacy teams, task forces, and other ways that the department could encourage controversy.

"Last but not least is the "reflect" group," Margaret said. "Reflecting is what we're doing, and we're learning that it can be fun and profitable. We need more sessions where we all get together away from the distractions of the office. Our group thought that we should do more patting each other on the back, making each one of us feel welcome and important.

"We need to take the time and take the risks to talk about our relationships, both the strengths and the weaknesses, and we need to be able to manage our conflicts. We're glad that we did that survey of managers because that helped us get a fix on what we could do and also let us know that we have to work together. As it is put in our readings, becoming a team organization is not a quick fix, but an ongoing effort and a journey."

After the discussion on reflecting, Russ said, "It's been a full day, and I want to use the last minutes to say a few words. First I want to thank everyone for getting involved. Let's pat each other on the back and give ourselves a round of applause for our good work today."

There were pats, cheers, and a few high-fives.

"As Margaret was saying, becoming a team is not done in a day, but we have lots of good ideas about how to proceed." Russ said. "I've taken detailed notes. Some of the things Angela and I can do, but most of them require all of us. We'll be getting back to you about proposals. I like what Dawn said about task forces, and perhaps we should form one that would find us tasks and rewards that would help us feel directed, united, and empowered."

"We'll also need to look at how we work with other managers," Rosalie said. "We have plenty of things to do."

"We have plenty of things to look forward to," Byron added. "I'm sure others want to join me in thanking Russ and Angela for going out on a limb and arranging this day for us." With that and with applause the meeting ended.

Margaret was laughing to herself about Lu's arguing that she was wrong about his numbers. How often had she heard managers tell her that? But she did not let herself become perturbed and saw an opportunity to work as a team with a manager. She asked Lu to stop by so that they could discuss his financial situation.

Lu was the supervisor of congregate elderly apartment complexes for the northwestern region of PMG. The Jubilee Apartments were the crown jewel of his organization, but they faced intense competitive pressures with new complexes coming on the scene and offering premiums and discounts to attract seniors to lease. Lu was under pressure to maintain occupancy rates and to reduce costs.

"I thought we're supposed to be a team here at PMG," Lu said. "Didn't I hear that someplace? But I ask for some help on marketing and they turn me down."

"We are a team, or at least we want to be," Margaret said. "I'd like to work with you to see if we can reduce costs and improve services together."

Lu's mood softened some, but he was still upset. "I'm supposed to go back to the staff and tell them that they are all supposed to get the place leased and work harder, and with any luck they will be able to work harder still and probably for less money. Sometimes the top people forget that they may have grand schemes, but we're the ones who have to implement them."

Margaret was learning not to take Lu's ventilating personally. Lu was letting off steam, and Margaret recognized that Lu had a difficult position linking management with workers. After Lu had vented some more, Margaret said reassuringly, "I don't think they intend to make our lives harder, but they face the reality of paying the mortgage every month, and with property values not rising they figure they need occupancy up, costs down, and rents stable. I hope that together we can come up with a plan for some way to do that."

"I appreciate that," Lu said, and they settled down to trying to come up with a plan. There did not appear to be any easy solution.

"I was thinking that making the four people at Jubilee more of a team might be the way to go," Lu offered. "They could help each other out and make life better for the residents, and they could help us reduce costs. The trouble is that Trent and the rest do not seem to get along. I hate to tell you how much time I waste listening to them complain about each other. Getting them together to come up with ways of keeping occupancy up and costs down might not be easy."

"I guess they aren't much of a team now," Margaret commented.

"That's right, although in a way they are." Lu said. "They help each other out, spend time together, and generally are quite cordial. The trouble is that Lorraine has the rest of them aligned against Trent."

"What's her problem with Trent?" Margaret asked.

"He's seen as too much of a goody-goody. He wants to do this differently, and he's got this idea and that idea. They won't talk to the guy. He's not sure what to do, so he runs to me, which makes the others even more angry."

"But we need people with ideas. Are any of his ideas good ones?" Margaret asked.

"He's inexperienced, but some of his ideas are worth pursuing. Lu added, "It's the way he brings them up that makes the others reject them out of hand. Perhaps—I just thought of this—the problem is that he is too oriented toward management."

"The more you talk, the more I see a need for a team approach at Jubilee." Margaret said. "All this bickering distracts us from making progress."

"Teamwork would be nice and would improve my life greatly," Lu admitted. "Certainly they could come up with better ideas to improve service than the marketing group lays on us. That 'smile more' program insulted the employees and was dead on arrival. But can they really become a team? Mistrust of management is a long tradition among workers. That is one thing they'll be solid about."

"Remember, though, that Frank Kincaid at the union likes this team organization idea," Margaret said.

At a future meeting, Margaret and Lu worked out a plan. Lu would introduce the idea of teamwork to the staff as a useful tool for them as people and for the company. They would have more opportunities and more responsibilities, and the company would benefit from having employees who contributed more and were more fulfilled. It was the more for more solution; staff would give more and get more. Lu reminded them that the union supported this idea, and he scheduled an afternoon session away from Jubilee.

Lu was coming to realize how much the distance between himself and the workers had grown. It was not intentional on his part; he had promised himself he would keep in touch with employees when he was promoted. He was intent on closing the distance, but he did not want to promise too much. He led off the afternoon workshop with his commitment to work more closely with the staff. "I've always thought I had an open door, but that may be hard to see from Jubilee. I want to be around more, know your concerns, answer your questions, and let you know where I am coming from. It is okay if you don't believe me completely. I want you to believe me when I come through."

Lu also talked about the value of teamwork for Jubilee, the residents, and staff. He handed out financial information, discussed the competitive pressures facing Jubilee, and talked about management's conclusion that it was vital to keep occupancy up and costs down. "I know that none of you have had much specific information before, and we can be criticized for that. But it was only when we were confronted with this tough situation that we understood how important it was to involve you all fully. In the old days, we never got too worried about occupancy and costs because property values were going up so much that we thought we were making money. The old days are gone."

Lu gave a brief overview of the team organization model; he had already handed them reading material on the model earlier. They discussed the model, and Lu emphasized that teamwork did not mean that everyone always agrees, but they must look at their conflicts and try to manage them.

After he had broken the staff into pairs and put Lorraine and Trent in the same one, Lu asked them to brainstorm about guides and rules for how they should work as a team. Then they discussed the two group's ideas and came up with a list:

"We are for the residents of Jubilee."
"Use 'we,' not just 'I.'"
"Ask people, don't force your ideas."
"Talk with the people you have a problem with, don't gossip behind their backs."
"Make work fun and interesting."

"I always thought that we couldn't be that much for each other because that would detract from our service to the residents," Pearl said. "But now I see that is just not the case. The better we are to each other, the better we can be for the residents."

"I enjoy my work now, but it would be nice to come to work feeling at one with everyone here," Davy said. "Most of us have problems outside of work with family and all, and it would be good to feel relaxed at Jubilee."

"And if we feel at home, the residents will feel at home," Pearl said.

"Are we ready to deal with our ongoing conflicts?" Lu asked. "Are we ready to bury the hatchet?"

"We could try," Lorraine said.

"We haven't heard from you, Trent," Lu said.

"I hope so," Trent answered.

Lu thought that he should build on the momentum. "Let's arrange a time when the three of us can get together and talk about the tension between the two of you and in the group."

"You mean 'team,' don't you?" Davy said with a laugh.

Lu had Lorraine and Trent review the material on the "reflect" part of the team organization model and then talk directly to each other about the conflict and frustrations that divided them. Trent was self-righteous at first. He said he felt ganged up on when he was only trying to do his job. But Lorraine pointed out that his "I'm right" attitude came through very clearly, but she was not convinced that he had been wronged. She thought he brought on his problems himself. He seemed to want to show up the group with Lu.

From there, they debated their views strongly. Lu broke in and had them rephrase the other's arguments until each person thought they were being understood. Lu then had them brainstorm about possible ways they could end the conflict. It was clear that it would take more time and work, but they did agree that they needed to talk to each other, not complain to Pearl, Davy, and certainly not to Lu.

The meeting was successful in helping each of them begin to see the problems from the other's standpoint. They also recognized that neither was intentionally hurtful and that both wanted a resolution and a good work relationship. They also saw that they all contributed to the conflict. Lorraine recognized that her isolating Trent made him more officious and more likely to run to Lu. Trent recognized that his self-righteousness showed and drove away Lorraine. And Lu recognized that he kept it going by supporting Trent and allowing them to avoid discussing issues with each other.

A week after meeting with Lorraine and Trent, Lu asked the workers to get their ideas together in preparation for a three-hour meeting to discuss and decide on how as a team they could contribute to quality service that would keep occupancy up and to practices that would keep costs down.

This meeting did not resolve the competitive pressures facing Jubilee, not did it result in many tangible decisions. That would take time. But there were encouraging signs. The workers got into the discussion and debated freely. Lu thought that they were actually better at mixing it up than were managers at PMG. There were some straightforward ideas that could be implemented right away. Lorraine could let her assistant help set up tables and serve people on Sunday nights to speed up service. Davy would not have to hire another person for those hours.

While it was fun to see these solutions identified and implemented, Lu was most excited about the long-term prospects. The workers agreed that they had to be more flexible in doing their duties and share tasks when necessary. They understood that each one could help residents in small, but meaningful ways. If someone saw a resident struggling with bringing in groceries, he or she could offer a hand even if it was not in the job description. Because her family was out of town, Lorraine said she was willing to celebrate some holidays at Jubilee to let the residents who had not left for the holidays know that the staff cared. Near the end of the meeting Davy said, "Let's make sure every resident feels wanted and valued."

Driving home that night, Lu felt released from the scrimmages of the past. He said to himself, "It'll be lots more fun debating over how we can do the best job possible rather than blaming and feeling mistrusted. And the staff and the residents will feel at home."

Challenging the "Mind Your Own Business" Approach

Since the early theorists Frederick Taylor and Henri Fayol, managers have assumed that individuals were the basic building blocks of an organization. But as Russ, Lu, and others were realizing, the individualistic milieu disrupts productivity and people, and using the team as the basic building block is a viable alternative.

The Limits of Individualistic Climates

The individual-based organization devises tasks small enough for an individual to accomplish alone, selects people with the abilities to do those tasks, provides needed resources, and asks supervisors to deal with unplanned events.

Russ saw his job as liaising with others in the organization and assigning tasks to individuals; he expected each member of the department to work on assigned tasks. The accountants and staff at PMG used this individualistic framework with some success. They demonstrated their professional abilities and autonomy and took pleasure in accomplishing their jobs and fulfilling their roles well. This approach worked well enough that it had continued for years.

Nevertheless the individualistic approach was not suited to cope with contemporary, intensive needs for accounting services at PMG. Managers wanted accounting information to make business decisions. Whereas four-month-old reports might have been good enough in the past, they were not enough today. New computer technology opened up possibilities for more timely and complete data, and managers wanted the accounting group to deliver. Lu and other managers also wanted the company's accountants to explain their financial situation and help them plan how to improve their performance.

As the tasks had become more complex and the skills of the people more varied, Russ was less able to provide monitoring and support. Nor could Russ call on one person to fill in when people were absent from the job. Managers were frustrated that when someone was sick or on leave, they could find no one to answer their questions. Department members also needed to turn to each other for assistance and ideas to keep current on new accounting practices. Employees at Jubilee could help each other learn the human and technical skills to become a first-class congregrate apartments.

Although completing tasks is a source of pride, a highly individualistic approach hurts people. It works against natural desires to be with other people and to share individual experiences and ideas. Prolonged independent work becomes impersonal, isolating, and potentially results in feelings of unimportance and rejection. Without cooperative links, people often begin to compete to show they are better than others. The formal organization stipulates independent work but is in fact competitive and debilitating.

Teams for Innovation

Team effort generates the commitment and capabilities to innovate. It does little good for an individual manager or employee to want to improve customer service, reduce costs, and introduce new technology unless others do too. For innovation to happen, employees and managers must be committed to the organization's taking the long-term perspective, gathering the courage, and persisting over hurdles to innovate.

North American businesses have been criticized, especially in comparison to Japanese firms, as being too narrowly focused on reducing labor costs. Managers make their mark by introducing a new technology that requires fewer workers or that employees work harder. The message businesses communicate is that workers are a drain on the company.

However, employees can be irreplaceable allies in creating valued-added products. In service industries it is widely recognized that the service providers—bank tellers, health-care professionals, retail clerks, hotel receptionists, cashiers—are critical for providing quality service and developing a competitive advantage. But employee commitment and innovation on the shop floor are also needed for innovation in manufacturing.

Getting Committed to Change

Russ began to realize that the "everyone do his own thing" way of working weakened the accounting group's efforts to be productive, respected, and an asset to the division. Instead of simply explaining his reasoning and announcing his plans, Russ worked to have the department members confront the reality of their situation and understand the need for change themselves.

Department members got feedback about the service they provided their "customers." This direct information challenged their original, defensive view that managers resented the accountants' unpleasant, but necessary task of controlling them. To make this feedback more dramatic, manager "customers" could have been invited to talk about their attitudes and feelings about the accountants face-to-face.

A complementary approach would have been for the accountants to reflect on their work relationships. They could complete questionnaires, be observed in meeting, and be interviewed so that they could better understand how people in the department perceive and feel about how they work together. The department could review these results, compare them with what they wanted, and make plans to strengthen their relationships.

Finding an Alternative

The department had to see an alternative before it would be keen about changing. It is not enough to wail against the imperfections of the present approach, because all approaches have shortcomings. Russ had to help his workers see that the team organization was a practical, viable alternative. Team organization must be understood to be something that not only pays off for the company and people but also can be done.

Russ's approach to the team organization program gave it credibility. Through discussion, consultation, and a highly interactive workshop, department members were acting as a team. They were gaining experience and confidence that as a team they were facing reality, identifying problems, and creating and implementing solutions.

Russ cannot create a team organization for the accounting department by himself. The members themselves must be involved. As operating a team organization requires the heart as well as the head and hands, so, too, does creating one. When the department members themselves understand the need, believe they have an alternative, and are confident that they can create a team organization, they are empowered and motivated.

Applying the Team Organization Model

Managers and employees must work together to create teams that are good for employees and for the company. Management attention and forming self-managing teams are only the first steps. Like other teams, employee groups need to envision a motivating goal, feel united and empowered, and be capable of exploring different views and reflecting on their progress.

Envision

The vision and goals of the employee team should clearly link self-interests to team effectiveness. Employees feel most energized when they clearly see how employee teams will fulfill their meaningful aspirations. Managers and employees have to break out of the traditional "either/or thinking" about the inevitable trade-offs between company and employee welfare. While there are opposing interests, overall the company requires energized and innovative employees; employees need a well-structured company so that they can contribute, feel secure in their jobs, and be respected.

To create this vision, managers must credibly communicate that they are committed to employee teams for the value they lend workers as well as the company. For Merchant and other companies, when union leaders support the team organization, employees are reassured that their leaders are working to ensure that these teams are structured to further and protect employee interests. Debating the value of employee teams can help employees understand that their investment in them is reasonable and potentially fulfilling.

Unite

Like other groups, employees will be more productive and enhanced when they believe they are on each other's side. The greater challenge is to have employee teams believe they are united with management. Traditional "us against them" industrial labor climates must be confronted and replaced with a team approach.

As managers and union leaders communicate their support for employee teams, they show that they believe the teams unite workers with each other and with management. The emphasis is on how managers and employees are together a team and will together share in the financial and emotional rewards as well as the burdens of their cooperative effort. Symbolic rewards such as parking spaces and common entrances can be revamped to communicate "we-ness" and "equality." Company or divisionwide bonus and gain sharing programs give credibility to these symbolic rewards. Individuals and teams are recognized for their contributions to their collective success. Excessive differences in salaries and executives who continually promote themselves as single-handedly saving the company disrupt feelings of unity.

Empower

Employees must feel empowered. They need to believe that they have the procedures, resources, and skills to make use of their opportunities. They require times and places to discuss issues, the administrative skills to set up and prepare for meetings, and the leadership abilities to develop their relationships, communicate effectively, and reach group consensus decisions. Individuals will have to be held accountable for accomplishing their assignments and contributing to the group. Team leaders and members need to discuss issues, to participate in workshops, and to help each other learn the many skills of working together as a team.

Explore

Exploring issues through discussing opposing views contributes to the success of employee teams. It is then that they dig into issues and innovate. They foster the right of dissent, listen to each other's arguments, and open-mindedly create solutions based on the best ideas. They brainstorm ideas, hash out proposals, and create solutions.

Reflect

Employee teams need ongoing reflection and renewal. Workers who have been on the assembly line for ten years have not automatically developed the vision, unity, and skills needed to work as a team. They have to experiment with procedures and skills to become more proficient and to find the ones that fit their situation. Teams need to set aside a time at their regular meetings to take stock of their relationships and productivity. They can meet off the shop floor periodically to reflect in depth on their present situation and make plans for strengthening their team and their innovation.

Developing work teams is a concrete way of giving today's employees the respect, involvement, and participation they demand and the opportunities to develop needed conceptual, technical, and social skills. Properly structured and managed, work teams further the learning of employees and the innovation of the firm. How employee teams develop this kind of effectiveness depends upon their situation and personalities, but the team organization guides managers and employees to form and to use their teams.

Through a team department, people can feel fulfilled by superior achievement, feel proud that they are serving their customers well, and feel supported and accepted. They have a commitment to challenging vision and goals, feel united behind this vision, and want to continue to explore issues. Department members empower and recognize each other's resources and reflect upon and share the credit for their success. In this way, individual employees feel successful and fulfilled, strengthen their self-confidence, and are prepared to keep working together to overcome obstacles and meet future challenges.

PART THREE

Achieving Synergy

Committed to spirited, lively teamwork as their approach, managers and employees are prepared to put team organization to work to get things done and strengthen their organization. Progress toward the team organization is a realistic, inspiring aspiration. Managers and employees can live with and often thrive upon difficulties and imperfections if they know where they want to go and believe they can get there. They feel powerful to change what needs to be changed. They are proud of their accomplishments and the distance they have travelled. A problem-free life is neither realistic nor desirable

Failure to make progress, on the other hand, demoralizes managers and employees. If the organization is not keeping up with the market and changes, it is falling behind. People feel powerless to do much about frustrations, hope that issues will go away, and look elsewhere for success. Yet most important frustrations do not melt away but remain around to distract and disillusion.

Organizations demand solutions to problems that integrate various perspectives. Chapter 9 details implications of the team organization model for structuring and working in a multidiscipline task force and project team. Team organization requires ongoing commitment and work, not an intensive one-week blitz. Chapter 10 explores the use of collegial support teams so that managers can help each other refine teamwork and leadership skills. Companies, even competitors, often collaborate in marketing and manufacturing arrangements and joint ventures. How team organization can be applied across organizations is discussed in chapter 11. Finally, chapter 12 reviews why and how you can continue to invest in your team organization.

Task Forces and Project Teams

*Loyalty to a petrified opinion never yet broke a chain or freed a human
soul.*

—*Mark Twain*

Skepticism is the first step toward truth.

—*Denis Diderot*

Brian took advantage of formal meetings and chance encounters
to convey his excitement about progress at PMG. He talked about
how people were coming together, helping, and lifting each other's
spirits. Some people did not share this assessment. They thought
that the slips, problems, and conflicts foreshadowed failure. Brian
saw them as inevitable signs of growth and change. He urged
doubters not to expect perfection or get distracted by momentary
mishaps, but to work for ongoing improvement.

Brian saw limitations as well. As he told Martin at lunch, he
couldn't help thinking that the program had made the lives of his
people better than his own. His relationships with his boss and others in the top management team were more superficial than he
would have liked. Sometimes the team would veto a division's plan
or impose a restriction. Brian was embarrassed that he could not
always defend the decision or its processes to his people though he
did not want to come across as back stabbing top management.
He'd say, "Sometimes there are things we just have to live with."

At Martin's urging, Brian resisted the temptation to withdraw
from the top management team to focus more on the division. Martin argued that his people depended upon him to keep up good
links with the top management. Withdrawal would buy short-term
comfort at the risk of long-term failure.

Brian recommitted himself to keeping up his relations with other division leaders and to seeing whether PMG and team organization could have more impact on Merchant. He saw the proposed high-tech park as an opportunity for people from his division to work with the development division. Stan Nakino, the head of the development division, teased Brian about teamwork: "We have a team looking at the new high-tech park, but a team is not going to solve the problems with that project. There are limits to teamwork, you know."

"I know," Brian answered trying not to sound annoyed. It struck him as very naïve for people to assume that he and other proponents of teamwork thought otherwise. That teams were sometimes ineffective and were not magical answers to problems was so obvious that it didn't warrant much discussion. But he did not want to get into a discussion of who was the most naïve. "I've heard that the project is back on hold again. What's up?" he asked Stan.

Stan explained that companies were very reluctant to sign leases, and Merchant needed eight solid commitments before they could go ahead with actual construction. "You know these high-tech guys—when times are great they spend big. We'll have to wait for another boom. That might be a while, I'm afraid, and we're going to have to keep paying the mortgage on all that expensive land."

"I've got an idea," Brian said. "Let us join you in developing the project." He explained that traditionally PMG had to finish leasing buildings, maintain them, and keep them going after the projects had been developed. "Take the Morgan High-Tech Park. Granted, it looks impressive, and companies wanted these monuments for buildings, but they're so expensive to heat and clean. And once the highflyers are gone, the professional manager or receiver, or whoever replaces them, considers the monuments signs of how the highflyers went wrong. The high-tech companies leasing from us now have a very different attitude. They are looking for value and for buildings on a human scale."

"I didn't realize that someone so much into teamwork would want to grab power," Stan teased.

"Love that power, but we want collective, team power." Brian wanted to address any concerns Stan had. "We don't want to tell you how to do your business, but we think we can be helpful partners."

"How would this happen?"

"A couple of people from leasing and maintenance would join your people to form a task force or project team" Brian suggested. "As a team they could try to come up with a workable proposal for the land. We would then respond to that proposal and have them answer our questions and concerns. When we have an idea we all believe in, we would approach Charles."

In selecting people, Stan and Brian aimed for diversity and re-sourcefulness. Diversity added depth and breadth of knowledge; the solution should reflect the perspectives of development, archi-tecture, construction, leasing, and maintenance. People from these groups would better understand the logic behind the decision and be more willing and able to implement it.

Brian and Stan wanted the interdivisional project team to begin with some fanfare. They invited members to a luncheon to meet socially and so they would see that Brian and Stan took this project seriously. Then Brian talked about the challenge to work together to make the new high-tech park a valuable addition to Merchant.

"But remember, the worse scenario is for us to build without leas-ing up quickly, and in this market that is possible," Stan warned. "So we do not look at a recommendation to sell the land as a bad decision. It may be the very smartest thing to do and we need to be smart today."

"Stan and I look forward to considering your ideas, and we trust that together you will dig into the issues and help us get a handle on what we should do," Brian said. "We know you have the individual abilities and expertise to be successful. The first thing we want you to do is to consider yourself a team. We have been using the team organization model in PMG and we recommend it as a guide for how your team can be effective. Armed with that understanding, we're confident that you can put your heads together and come up with a sound plan that we can believe in and defend to Charles."

Most project teams understand the need for administrative work such as finding convenient meeting times and places and dividing up the work and deciding who is responsible for what parts of the project. Much less is done to develop relationships and make the norms and procedures of working together explicit. The hope is that the team members will naturally jell into a cohesive group.

Failing that, a consultant might have to be hired to pick up the pieces and repair the team.

Brian wanted the team to avoid this pattern. Stan agreed that the project leader should be familiar with the team organization model. They selected Marilyn from the PMG division to be the project leader and briefed her about how she could begin work on forming the project team and using the team organization model to develop explicit guides.

Marilyn told the project team, "Those of us from PMG have more experience with team organization, but we're not trying to use our knowledge to get a leg up on you. We recognize that we can only be successful if all of us understand and buy into the team-work idea. According to the model, we can only be successful if we empower each others."

With Marilyn directing, project team members did a modified jigsaw approach to learning the model. One pair learned the reflect and vision parts of the model, another pair focused on unity, and a third took empower and explore. After the pairs had discussed and learned their assigned parts, they summarized and taught each other.

After a discussion about the model and a debate on its merit, the team developed the following guidelines and procedures:

Our focus is on creating the best possible plan for Merchant, not on what is best for development or PMG.

We all take credit; we all take responsibility.

We support each other inside and outside the group.

We treat each other with respect and listen to each other's ideas.

We show our confidence in each other.

We open-mindedly consider each other's ideas and don't take disagreement as a personal attack.

When we have problems and frustrations with someone, we talk directly to that person or, if appropriate, bring it up at a group meeting.

Gossiping and secret alliances are unacceptable.

"This is a good list to begin with," Marilyn said. "We can build upon and redefine it as we go."

"The biggest challenge for us is to be able to discuss our opposing views constructively," Alnoor said. "We represent some very different perspectives."

"It almost seems like we have different languages and values, " Preston added.

"That's a good thing and a bad thing, " Dave said. "It is a problem and an opportunity."

"That's why this cooperative unity is so important," Marilyn said. "It gets us oriented to how we can understand and build upon each other rather than decide who is better and who is right."

"Sounds good," Dave said. "But the question is how can we pull this off? How can this constructive controversy actually be carried out?"

Marilyn proposed her plan for using advocacy teams to begin exploring the New High-Tech Park. She would divide them into two groups. One group would be assigned the position that Merchant should build a high-tech park on the land, the other group the position that Merchant should sell the land and cut its losses. Each group would have a day to review all the documents and information already collected on the project and develop all the arguments they could that supported their position. They were free to bring whatever sources or information they could find inside and outside the firm. Marilyn added with a smile, "Unfortunately, we do not allow actually making up data."

"Are you accusing us marketing types?" Dave said, feigning insult.

"I thought she was talking to construction," Helen said.

Marilyn handed out the procedures for advocacy teams and explained that after they had prepared their arguments, they would argue their views face-to-face. Each side would present its arguments and then debate freely. Each group would have to restate the other group's position fully. Then they would drop their assigned views and try to reach a consensus.

The debate was full, loud, and energizing. The overall conclusion was not surprising: Merchant should try to build the park. The debate got everyone familiar with the situation and up to speed: they would not need to reinvent the wheel. The team was critical of some previous assumptions and assumed risks. The "sell the land" group had convincingly identified potential pitfalls that their proposal would have to address seriously.

"I've kept track of the risks and pitfalls of developing the site," Marilyn said. "We should refer to this list as we develop our plan and come back to it to critique our proposal before we present it to Stan and Brian."

"I hope this is not the last of these advocacy teams and controversy," Preston said. "It was fun and worthwhile."

"We have just begun," Marilyn said. "I can see us having lots of little debates as we discuss various points and go through problem-solving steps. We could also have more advocacy teams. we might decide, for example, that before we send our proposal to Stan and Brian, we'll want to form 'Build this proposed project' and 'Scrap the proposed project' advocacy teams."

Three months later, project team members were excited and confident about presenting their proposal. They thought they had the elusive combination of the creative and the practical. The park would look different and function well; it would work for the clients and for Merchant.

Marilyn had given Stan and Brian advanced notice; the team did not want to catch them off guard. But this was the team's chance to explain and defend its proposal fully. Rather than Marilyn presenting the proposal by herself, all team members were involved.

Based on their discussion with high-tech firms and their internal debates, they proposed an integrated high-tech park. A growing number of small, niche high-tech firms saw themselves as quite dependent on other firms. But rather than attempt to carry out various functions within a large company, these niche firms chose to be separate and highly specialized. For example, some focused solely on research and development (R&D). Because a new product might last only six months, success in the computer world required continuous upgrading of products. To put new products into production quickly, R&D firms needed strong links with manufacturing specialists. Manufactured products needed access to efficient marketing channels. Staying on top in the high-tech industry meant a great deal of collaboration across firms. They had to know, trust, and rely on each other to make their specialized capabilities jointly productive.

The proposed high-tech park would facilitate this collaboration. Underground cables would reliably and efficiently link buildings electronically. The buildings and common spaces would be on a human scale with no expensive, awe-inspiring atriums or imposing, overbearing offices. Buildings would be situated around common facilities and park area. People from the different firms could meet regularly for tennis and racquetball, walks, and meetings. The common facilities could hold company picnics: many high-tech workers had children, so picnics were replacing Friday afternoon "beer busts."

"Nothing wrong with grand ideas, and I've come up with a few in my youth," Stan said. "I don't mean to rain on your parade, but I've seen so many contemporary plans become expensive white elephants. Whenever I see something unusual like this, I keep asking, "Who's going to buy this and help pay the mortgage?"

That's a reasonable question we asked ourselves," Alnoor said. "We believe that the high-tech firms themselves will help us. Companies already have links, and they want their partners to move with them. The firms are not large, but we believe they will come in groups."

After more discussion, Brian proposed that the project team be given a budget to develop the plans further, including preparing a scale model and approaching high-tech firms to gauge their interest. After two months, they would meet again and review how many firms were ready to make commitments to the project.

"I like the concept," Stan said. "But I would feel a lot better about arguing for it strongly if we had more concrete evidence about its marketability."

"We need to be cautious as we innovate, if that makes sense," Brian said.

"Makes sense," Alnoor said. "We have come to believe in the idea, but we know we can't be blindly committed to it."

"It will be fun getting information about just how valid our idea is," Dave added.

Exploring Opposing Views to Solve Problems

Solving problems is the *sine qua non* of an effective organization. In solving problems, people exploit new opportunities and use frustrations to learn to become more effective. Without problem solving the organization loses direction, becomes demoralized, and common goal are lost in laying blame. But decision makers must negotiate several steps and overcome many barriers to be successful.

Studies document that in identifying and analyzing the problem, creating alternatives, and considering and selecting the final option individuals are closed to new and opposing information, fail to evaluate information adequately, and have an unwarranted confidence in their conclusions. For example, they often dismiss information that opposes their point of view, simplify the relevant consequences to be considered, and use early trends to draw conclusions prematurely. Despite the tendency to commit these errors of judgment, individuals have been found to be quite confident they are right.[1]

It cannot be assumed that people are able to identify their goals clearly, search for all available alternatives, predict the consequences of implementing each of these alternatives, and finally choose the one that best promotes their original goals. Decision makers cannot be expected to know where they want to go, to recognize and be able to consider all possible approaches, and then dispassionately to select the best.

However, as other studies document, and as the high-tech project team discovered, people working together can negotiate the different aspects of problem solving.[2] They can explore issues and combine ideas, and they can gain the confidence and power necessary to see new developments as opportunities, not threats.

Leaders and team members must ensure that they have the structures, procedures, and skills to solve problems together so that they can express their opposing views openly and constructively. Through productive controversy, team members doubt their own position, ask questions to explore alternatives, take opposing information seriously, develop a more accurate view of the situation, and incorporate opposing positions into their own thinking and decisions.

Harmony is much lauded, but avoiding controversy undermines decision making. When team members suppress their differences, they can make poor decisions that threaten the credibility and vitality of the company. They remain ignorant of risks and opportunities and make decisions without thoughtful analyses. They court disaster as well as stagnation. Productive controversy helps teams and organizations deal with the complex, varied demands of solving problems and making decisions.

Problem-Solving Steps

The high-tech park project team used controversy to develop ground rules for its dynamics, to define the problem, to dig into the issues, to create alternatives, to evaluate and decide, and to recommend their solution to management. Through productive controversy, team members can create an innovative, but practical solution.[3]

Forming a Team Organization Framework

Brian and Marilyn wanted the project team to begin by setting norms for strong relationships and procedures to follow. Team members learned about the team organization model and then discussed and debated it. The model could not be decreed, but needed to be understood and believed in before it could guide the team. Team members made rules and norms explicit, not because they would always follow them, but because they could use rules and norms as a guide. When conflicts and frustrations occurred, they could refer to the norms as reminders about how they wanted to work together.

Defining the Problem

There are three major steps to defining a workable problem: (1) create an ideal, but attainable state of affairs; (2) determine the present state of affairs; and (3) compare the ideal to the present to identify the discrepancy.

The project team discussed what would be an ideal state of affairs: they wanted a project that would promote the interests of all groups at Merchant. The project would have to be developable, constructible, marketable, and maintainable. It was not enough for the project to look good for development. It had to work for the whole company and for the long term. They also gathered information about the present state of affairs. They analyzed the plot of land and its characteristics. They critiqued the proposed plans for the land. Then they compared the present and the future state and realized that a great deal of thought was needed in developing a project that would be attractive to clients while keeping risk and maintenance costs at manageable levels.

Suggestions for defining the problem include:

1. List statements that describe the problem as concretely as possible. The team reviews the list and adds as much as possible.
2. Restate the problem so that it contains both the present and the ideal state of affairs. Define the problem so that it is solvable and urgent.
3. Describe thoroughly the benefits to the team and the organization of solving the problem. What will the company look like after the problem is solved?

Defining the problem is critical because it provides the motivating vision for the team. An ill-defined problem can lead team members to take an unproductive, frustrating path leaving them feeling directionless and powerless. It is worth time and controversy to define the problem so that people are inspired, directed, and empowered.

Digging into the Problem

The project team used advocacy teams to examine the nature and magnitude of the problem. They gathered information about it, became more aware of the major roadblocks and pitfalls they faced, and saw opportunities they could exploit. One group proposed selling the land as a way to critique present assumptions and preliminary plans for the site. That proposal helped them question common conclusions, see the inadequacies of traditional thinking, and break out of the mold.

Force field analysis can be used to examine the forces that are acting upon a problem and has long been used in the diagnosis of social and organizational issues.[4] The present is defined as a quasi-stationary equilibrium, a balance of contending forces—some pushing toward and some pushing away from the more desired state of affairs.

As Figure 9–1 indicates, the helping forces are pushing on the current state of affairs to move them toward the more desired state, but the restraining forces are pushing the current situation toward a worse state. The present situation will improve if the restraining forces are weakened or the helping forces are strengthened. As strengthening helping forces typically pressures and engenders resistance, reducing the restraining forces is often more practical and effective.

For example, a leader interested in developing a team organization might have the team brainstorm about all the helping and restraining forces. Helping forces include recognizing that teamwork furthers innovation and improves the quality of work life, building the confidence that people can communicate openly and work as a team, and training the team in conflict management skills. Restraining forces are pressures to perform in the short term, commitment to posturing, uncertainties about what team organization is, and doubts that the team has the skills and procedures to work together. With this kind of analysis, the team is more prepared to create and evaluate alternative solutions.

Creating Solutions

Decision makers are often too fixed on a narrow range of possibilities. They may grab on to the first solution mentioned, or the one

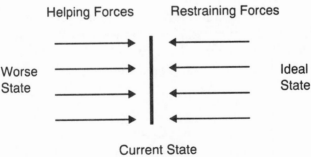

FIGURE 9–1
Force Field Analysis

proposed by the person with the highest status. Sometimes they are locked into "either/or" thinking or the belief that they need a "compromise" solution in the "middle."

The analysis of helping and restraining forces facilitates creating a variety of ways to solve the problem. Decision makers recognize that there are a number of forces acting on the problem, and they can intervene through them. Rather than rely on one approach, they develop a plan that incorporates action on a number of different factors. For example, group members interested in becoming a team organization can read and discuss the advantages of teamwork, share their conviction that they want to work together, practice negotiation and controversy skills together, and develop task forces and project teams to facilitate collaboration.

Individual and group brainstorming in which people put forth many possible solutions to a problem can begin the process of creating alternatives. Here all ideas are accepted and listed no matter how unusual or impractical they may sound. In many groups, there is a strong tendency to evaluate and judge ideas quickly and dismiss those considered impractical. This tendency suppresses original thinking and rewards people for proposing traditional solutions whose rationales are well known.

Rules for brainstorming include:

1. Focus on one problem. Break complex problems into simpler ones that lend themselves to solutions.
2. Promote an open and relaxed atmosphere where everyone feels free to contribute.
3. Accept all ideas. Evaluation of the value of the ideas and their practicality is suspended.
4. Aim for quantity, not quality. The more ideas there are the more likely that eventually some will provide useful.
5. Build on each other's ideas. The suggestion of one helps others break out of traditional thinking and create new possibilities.
6. Record all ideas.

Constructive controversy builds upon brainstorming as the decision makers consider and debate new options. The exchange and clash of ideas, the doubts and uncertainties, and the interpersonal support and encouragement in productive controversy lead to divergent, creative thinking. It is through this kind of give-and-take that the project team was able to discard outworn ideas and begin to accept new ideas.

Evaluating Alternatives

Once a number of options have been identified, the decision makers need to analyze the advantages and disadvantages of each and determine the relative effectiveness of the options. The more explicit this evaluation is the more confidence people can have that the chosen option has greater advantages and benefits than disadvantages and costs. While the solution may not be optimal, it will be one that people believe is the best they could do.

Janis and Mann[5] proposed a procedure to facilitate vigilant analysis of alternatives. The problem-solving team evaluates each alternative on four criteria: (1) the tangible gains and losses for the team and company; (2) the tangible gains and losses for customers, investors, and other stakeholders; (3) intangible gains and losses in the self approval of team members and company employees; (4) intangible gains and losses in the self approval of significant others.

The problem-solving group then completes a balance sheet for each option. On one side, the group identifies the tangible gains and losses for the company and significant others, and on the other side the intangible consequences. Then they rate each item on a scale of one to ten, from no importance to extremely important. Using the balance sheet, the team ranks the solutions from the most to the least effective.

Constructive controversy helps in developing the information necessary to complete this balance sheet to identify the gains and losses. Team members need to debate and question each other so that they can arrive at reasonable predictions about the consequences of different options.

Making Decisions

Creativity and analysis need to be followed by decision. It is not enough to talk about the problem; the team has to make its judgment about the best course of action. The team members need to reach an agreement on the action most desirable for achieving the goals of the team and the company.

Decision making should of course lead to a high-quality solution. The course of action solves the underlying problem using the available resources and time and in such a way that it does not reoccur. But an effective decision must also bring about a commitment by those who are to implement it. An elegant decision does little good if implemented improperly or half-heartedly. Decision making should also be efficient so that the time and resources of the team are well spent. It is usually very desirable if the experience leaves the team with stronger relationships, more credibility within the company, and more skills for solving future problems.

Consensus is the method that typically results in the most effective resolutions to important problems, but it can be too time consuming for simple, unimportant issues. Consensus in a pure form implies that everyone is in total agreement on the course of action. More realistically, consensus means that instead of relying on a majority vote, all people are given an opportunity to be heard and to influence the decision. People who do not agree with the final group decision believe they have expressed their objection and are willing to commit themselves to the decision for a certain period.

The underlying reason for the importance of consensus is that it promotes constructive controversy. People speak their minds and defend their thinking. But they open-mindedly listen to others and change their minds based on arguments and reasons. The basic rules of consensus decision making are:

1. Express your own ideas clearly and logically, but avoid arguing blindly for them. Consider other viewpoints.
2. Change your mind based on the objective and logical arguments of others. Do not change your mind to avoid conflict.
3. Seek a consensus decision. Avoid majority voting, tossing a coin, and bargaining.
4. Foster opposing views. Encourage people to become involved and speak their minds.
5. Discuss underlying assumptions and ideas. State the rationales behind your position.
6. Strive for a win-win solution that incorporates the best of all ideas. Avoid thinking in terms of winning and losing.

7. Reconsider an earlier decision. Sometimes a team should have a "second chance" meeting in which team members express any remaining doubts and make changes so that they remain committed to the team's solution.

Proposing a Solution

For important decisions, problem-solving groups must help others understand their proposed solution and become committed to implementing it. Managers have to be confident so that they can commit the company's resources and credibility to the proposed project.

The team wants to define the problem, describe its proposed solution, and present its rationale as completely and as persuasively as possible. After making sure everyone understands the proposed course of action, the team indicates all the facts, arguments, and information that underlie it. The team develops a logical argument that includes a coherent structuring of ideas and information. The team makes its case sincerely and forcefully so that people will understand it and take the proposal seriously.

The team wants to be persuasive and forceful to engage the listeners, not so that they feel obliged to agree. Team members show confidence in themselves and their position and demonstrate their commitment to the best solution by inviting and encouraging debate and disagreement. Through controversy they can more thoroughly communicate the underlying rationale and remain open to modifying their recommendation in light of the information and arguments offered by people outside the team.

Stan and Brian argued and made objections to the project team's proposed park. After a group has made a proposal, small ad hoc decision-making groups can facilitate involvement and discussion. For example PMG and development people in groups of three can consider the task force's proposal for the park. Within each group, they debate whether to accept the proposal and, if not, what modifications they want. Then the groups share their conclusions and the large group makes a decision to accept or modify the proposal. (See chapter 6 for ad hoc decision-making group procedures.)

Implementing and Monitoring Solutions

Agreement on a high-quality solution must be followed with effective implementation. Typically, the problem-solving team will want to oversee the implementation to ensure the proposal has the opportunity to solve the problem. It develops a responsibility plan that outlines who is responsible for what tasks and a time line.

The team evaluates and makes judgments about the extent to which the solution has been implemented properly. It compares the actual implementation against the responsibility plan, identifies shortcomings, and works to implement the solution.

The team also wants to assess the impact of the implemented solution. If the current state of affairs has not been appreciably changed in the desired direction, the group needs to select a new solution and implement it. More generally, the team wants to analyze the present state of affairs to identify whether there are new problems that deserve attention. The solution to one problem often brings other problems into the open and makes them more salient and practical to deal with. Monitoring then should result in a new set of issues and concerns and initiate a new problem-solving sequence.

Advocacy Teams for Making Decisions

The best way ever devised for seeking the truth in any given situation is advocacy: presenting the pros and cons from different, informed points of view and digging down deep into the facts
—Harold S. Geneen, Former CEO, ITT

Managers often encourage conflict in decision making by asking everyone to speak their minds and telling it like it is. Structuring advocacy teams and assigning them different positions is a thorough way to develop constructive, controversial discussions that can help to define and analyze a problem as well as to create and evaluate alternatives.

Phase 1: A problem important enough to warrant the time and resources needed to explore it comprehensively is identified. Simple, unimportant problems do not deserve extensive exploration and take time and attention away from significant issues. Focusing on unimportant issues can be very demoralizing and frustrating.

Phase 2: Advocacy teams are formed and each one assigned a major alternative. The teams are given the time and resources to find all the supporting facts, information, evidence and reasons for their alternative. They plan how they can present their arguments so that everyone is well aware of the strengths of their position. Their goal is not to win the debate by getting their position accepted, but they still want to present their arguments forcefully and thoroughly so that their position will be seriously considered.

Phase 3: Teams present their arguments and positions fully and persuasively. In this free discussion, they develop their own arguments, advocate their position, defend them against refutation, and counter opposing arguments. They take notes and challenge inadequate facts and reasoning.

Phase 4: The teams open-mindedly listen and present each other's position. They rephrase each other's positions and arguments to demonstrate that they have paid attention and understand. Throughout the discussion, they remember the purpose is for the whole group to develop as strong a position as possible.

Phase 5: Teams together strive for an integrated decision. The subgroups drop their assigned position, and using all the facts and arguments that have been identified they reach a general agreement on the best course of action. They change their minds because of the logic and evidence, not because others are more powerful or argue more loudly. The decision reflects their best joint, reflected judgment.

Phase 6: The group as a whole approaches management and others to make and to implement their decision. Making a decision in an organization is more that getting the right answer. Decisions are not puzzles to be solved; they are part of the stream of working and managing. The solution must be accepted and implemented, its impact assessed, and new problems identified.

Phase 7: The group reflects on their use of conflict to make decisions. Though advocacy teams can be exciting, involving, and worthwhile, they are not easy. It can be tempting to fall back into the typical mode of trying to dominate and "win" by getting one's position accepted. Team members can easily get caught up in proving they were right and the other person was wrong. They have to remind themselves that what counts is not who was right at first but that the team is right at the end.

Problems test organizations. There are significant barriers that interfere with completing the complex steps of making a decision in an organization. It takes courage and confidence to deal with the unknown risks of new approaches.

Constructive controversy can unlock the power of team problem solving. Structuring businesses into family groups and exploiting the heterogeneous viewpoints and backgrounds within a corporation can rejuvenate products and services and help the corporation cope with intense competition.[6] During a crisis, decision makers may successfully cope by creating and then objecting to a series of positions.[7]

Guides for Advocacy Teams

Phase 1: Select a problem that warrants a comprehensive evaluation.
Identify the major alternative positions.

Phase 2: Assign teams opposing positions.
Provide resources for teams to gather arguments and information for their position.

Phase 3: Each team presents its arguments.
Listen open-mindedly and challenge constructively.

Phase 4: Teams rephrase the opposing arguments.
Put into your own words the ideas, logic, and facts of the other side.

Phase 5: The team as a whole strives for an integrated solution.
Examine all the evidence and arguments to reach a consensus decision.

Phase 6: The team implements the decision.
Persist and follow through with the agreement.

Phase 7: The team reflects and learns from its experience.
Discuss strengths and areas to improve.

It is through controversy that individuals help each other cope with the biases of closed-mindedness, simplistic thinking, inadequate evaluation of information, and unwarranted commitment to a position. Teams can use this conflict to understand opposing positions, develop alternatives, and integrate apparently disparate positions into creative, high-quality solutions.[8]

But not all controversy is useful because it needs to be discussed cooperatively and skillfully. The decision makers must understand that their opposing views do not mean that they have opposing goals and objectives.

Controversy tests teams. Teams need the values, skills, and procedures to make conflict positive. Team members must express their ideas forcefully but also be open to understanding other points of view. They dig into the issues to develop a complex understanding of the problem and incorporate various ideas into useful recommendations. They gain consensus and agreement through direct, open discussion of conflicting opinions.

Leader Development Teams

Wanting to lead and believing you can lead are only the departure points on the path to leadership. Leadership is . . . a performing art. And in the art of leadership, the artist's instrument is the self. The mastery of the art of leadership comes with the mastery of the self. Ultimately leadership development is a process of self-development.

—James Kouzes & Barry Posner, The Leadership Challenge

"I'm delighted about the project team on the new high-tech park," Anthony said. "Just the idea of working with the development population before we get their projects dumped on us is liberating."

"They're coming up with some interesting ideas for what we might do in this market," Brian said.

"Getting this project team going gives the team organization idea more credibility," Anthony said.

"Agreed. What do you think about our progress in becoming a team organization?" Brian asked.

"Good," Anthony responded. "People are excited, and I think knowledgeable. It means more to people than words and slogans. But translating all of it into action is difficult. Sometimes people like you and me see the logic of working together cooperatively so clearly that we don't see so clearly how much it can take to put it into place."

"In some ways it's so commonsense and everyday, but in other ways it is so different from the way we have been taught was the right way to manage," Brian said.

"Working as a team is, in a way, like coming back to the basis," Anthony mentioned.

"We need to help our managers keep the faith and keep working on their team organization. We've got to keep the momentum," Brian urged.

"Our managers want help." Anthony thought silently for a moment. "I like it when my managers come to me with questions about how to get people working as a team. That part is great, but responding to them is a problem. It can be very difficult thinking of something useful to say. I want to encourage them, but I'm not always able to help."

"One thing we talked about in my executive program was management development teams," Brian offered. "Interested managers would get together regularly to talk about their plans and problems in developing team organization."

Brian and Anthony discussed the purposes and activities of management development teams and decided to run the idea past the other managers. The management team gave their blessing and suggested that these teams be called "leader development teams." The managers agreed that it was important to concentrate on one support team and build upon its success.

Brian recognized that to make the first team successful he needed to have managers interested in and capable of developing teams and skilled at working with other managers. He asked people to suggest candidates and tried to think about managers who were particularly interested in team organization.

To give the group a profile and underscore its importance, Brian himself explained the idea to the selected managers. He urged them to consider joining, but if they chose not to he would not hold it against them because there would be future opportunities. One manager cited the expected birth of a child in declining; the four others agreed to meet next week.

Brian lead the first meeting and explained that he wanted to be available to the group and attend some of the sessions. "There may be times when you don't want me here! Seriously, your discussions are confidential, and sometimes you'll find they'll be more fruitful if you don't have to wonder how I or other members of the management team might react. But if you do have problems and conflicts with me, certainly I want us to talk directly."

Brian wanted them to meet for a full two hours to begin with, although future sessions would probably be shorter. His first major objective was for them to get to know each other as people, to develop trust, and to set the groundwork for making future sessions personal and fun. The second aim was to begin work on how they could help each other learn. Managers needed to leave their meetings with a sense of accomplishment as well as good feelings about the group.

After muffins and coffee, introductions, and a brief reminder of the purpose and activities of leader teams, Brian said, "We've been brought up to believe in 'macho' management. We're tough guys who can take the heat and make tough choices. We even take pride in how hard we work and how little sleep we get when we take leadership courses.

"Here we're trying to be sensitive team leaders and team members who involve the hearts as well as the heads and hands of our people, knock down barriers for them, and deal directly and compassionately with their problems and conflicts. A crash course is not going to do that for us. We need to learn from our experiences and from each other."

After questions and comments, Brian had the people who knew each other the least pair up and interview each other on their strengths as leaders and managers and the experiences that had helped them develop these strengths. They briefly reported what they had learned about the strengths of the person they interviewed. The managers had learned by watching and being encouraged by effective bosses, through conflict with colleagues, and occasionally by being determined not to lead in the same way as a destructive boss.

Brian had them switch partners and interview each other on how they wanted to improve their leadership capabilities. Each pair then reported its ideas, and Brian wrote them down on a flip chart. The group's major goals were to become more capable of managing conflict, to introduce team organization to employees, to deal with a competitive employee who wants no part of working as a team, to communicate consistently and credibly to employees, and to reduce political posturing and gossiping.

"These are all important goals," Brian said. "I want to emphasize that you can accomplish these goals much better by working together than by yourselves. We're not talking ideology here, we're talking practicality. You have an additional important shared mission: to lead the rest of the organization. I would love it if after six months I could point to this group as an example for other managers. You're the cutting edge and can model the way for the whole organization."

"I like that, but I hope you don't mind my being specific," Doris said. "Will we be attending seminars and having a budget?"

"I'll make some money available for refreshments and courses. You can share what you have learned from conferences and talks with each other. It would also be great if all of you attended the same course together."

"Rafting down the Colorado River!" Victor cried. "I'm ready."

"Something naturally flowing like the Colorado would fit in with your idea of not being 'macho,'" Doris continued the laughter.

"Didn't I say something about being an example to the rest of the organization?" Brian joined in the fun. "I was thinking more of a real winter survival exercise to show that you have to work together to make it out of the back country of Manitoba alive."

"We'll talk about whether we should add that to our goals and get back to you," Rod said. "We make decisions as a team here."

"I recognize that this leader team is more work and adds to your already busy schedule," Brian said. "Believe me, I don't want people to spend all their time at PMG. You've got family and friends and a life outside of here. But I believe that what you can learn here could be immensely beneficial to your as professionals and to your outside life. If done right, it'll be an investment that will continue to pay off for you and the rest of us."

Brian asked the managers to negotiate a contract. They agreed to meet once every two weeks for an hour and a half, they would take turns structuring the meetings and providing any readings or other materials and refreshments. In between sessions they would work on improving their leadership and teamwork skills and be prepared to discuss their progress at the next meeting. They would also visit each other's areas and be available between meetings as needed. They agreed that their goal was to help each other develop as people and leaders.

Empowering Leaders

Leaders are at the center of creating a team organization. They challenge misleading ideas and obsolete practices and show the way to forge a synergistic team. They begin the process of replacing posturing, self-protection, and conformity with genuine relationships, respect for all, and open give-and-take. They empower others to make a difference.

But leaders need to be empowered, too. To draw upon their values and capabilities and adjust to new opportunities, they turn to mentors and trusted peers for counsel. Becoming a leader requires continual nourishment throughout a lifelong journey. Professional support groups can help managers discuss issues and get the feedback and encouragement needed to experiment and persist.

Purposes and Value

Leadership, we have argued, is a "we" thing that managers and employees do together, but managers need each other, too. Leaders turn to each other to brainstorm steps to forge and renew their teams. They want to know how to extend teamwork to suppliers in a just-in-time delivery program or to a competitor so they can form a joint venture. To deal with complex conflicts, leaders need another perspective. Charges of unethical action or sexual harassment require sensitive, decisive action, and most prudent managers want to discuss their options with people they trust.

Development teams encourage the heart. Managers strengthen each other's courage and savvy to become effective team organization leaders. These support groups supplement formal education, leadership and teamwork courses, in-house development programs, and private discussions and help leaders apply their knowledge to concrete situations. Leader development teams help bridge the gap between ideas and application, between what leaders say and what they do.

In a leader development team, two to six managers meet regularly to talk about their efforts to create team organizations and strengthen their skills as leaders and people. They provide assistance, serve as an informal support group for sharing problems and letting off steam, allow more experienced leaders to serve as mentors and assistants, and foster shared camaraderie and success. Development teams are safe places where members like to be, where they experience support, caring, and laughter, and where they reinforce their determination to create team organizations.

The choice is not so much whether to have management support groups or not, but what their purpose and nature will be. In the absence of structured teams, managers form informal alliances. They join forces for self-protection and self-enhancement, even at the expense of others. Leader development teams focus managers on issues of personal and organizational long-term value, not on short-term survival and self-promotion.

Structuring leader development teams is a specific action and concrete symbol of the company's commitment to increasing the competence and well-being of people. One of the most inspiring and uniting reasons for team organization is that it promotes people. Everyone wins when people learn. Leader teams credibly demonstrate a company's commitment to self-development.

Leader Team Activities

Managers use their leader team to share information, celebrate successes, and solve problems.[1] Together they plan, design, and evaluate their efforts at creating team organization. They visit each other's offices and teams and provide feedback.

The teams foster professional discussions in which managers talk directly and honestly about the challenges, frustrations, and opportunities of leadership. They talk in increasingly concrete and precise terms about the nature of team organization and how it can be applied. They use their shared, precise language to describe team organization, to distinguish one practice and its virtues from others, and to integrate team organization with other ideas and approaches. Through discussing, explaining, and teaching they deepen their understanding and skills in teamwork.

Managers together plan programs and activities to strengthen their team organizations. They can develop programs that teach them to value and manage the diversity of people, and they can create a code of ethics. They can share the burden and excitement of being a leader and learn from others' experience. As they put team organization in place, they need to clarify their understanding of teamwork and get the encouragement needed to experiment with plans that are appropriate for their people and situations. Discussions about the effectiveness of previous attempts suggest how they can modify their plans for future action.

Managers observe and give each other feedback. Most managers are unsure of their impact on employees and believe that employees are reluctant to be direct and honest. Managers can visit each other's teams and give an outside, informed perspective on group dynamics and leadership. Observation and feedback should be reciprocal to reinforce the idea that everyone is helping each other learn. Of course, managers need to be respectful and, when pointing out shortcomings and problems, recognize that everyone has strengths and weaknesses and good and bad days.

Observing and Giving Feedback

Helpful Norms

1. We do not have to be perfect.
2. It takes time to be an effective team organization leader.
3. We are here to improve our abilities.
4. We don't take feedback as personal attacks.
5. We are secure enough to give feedback.

Guides

1. Recognize that you can learn about leadership by observing experienced and inexperienced managers.
2. Make observation and feedback reciprocal.
3. Ask the manager you are observing what he or she wants you to focus on.
4. Give feedback on actions and performance, not personal competence.
5. Separate the manager's personal worth from his or her success in using team organization.
6. Be concrete and practical.
7. Communicate respect for the manager's abilities and motivation.

Structuring Development Teams

Managers have an inspiring vision of promoting each other's human sensitivities and leadership abilities so that they can create the team organization for employees and the company. They have the cooperative, united goal to help each other become more competent. As one becomes more able, that helps others learn. As the more experienced manager teaches the less experienced, the more experienced manager learns too. They are empowering each other by sharing their ideas and work. They explore the meaning of team organization and discuss problems in its implementation. They reflect on their progress in becoming leaders and a team.[2]

Leaders like Brian need to work with and structure leadership teams. Because these groups have very important purposes, they cannot be allowed to degenerate into gripe sessions, amateur therapy groups, or alliances for playing office politics. Leaders can follow the guidelines listed under each part of the team organization model to form effective leader development teams.

Envision

1. *Show your support for team organization.* In talks, informal conversations, and newsletters leaders describe their conviction that the company should work as a team. They describe teamwork as vital to the company's success and publicly recognize concrete examples of team organization. They describe how team organization and leader teams in particular fit in with the broad direction of the company.

2. *Identify how leadership teams complement team organization.* Leaders explain to prospective members that these teams can help them study the nature of team organization, plan how to put it in place in their areas, and get ongoing feedback and assistance from each other. In this way, they can improve their leadership skills and help their population work together.

3. *Remind managers of the value of team organization and leadership skills.* The team organization helps employees

innovate, learn, and become committed to making the company one they can be proud of. Learning leadership skills helps managers become more open, flexible, and competent at work and at home.

Unite

1. *Show managers how they "sink or swim" together.* They need to help each other learn about team organization and develop a program and procedures that fit their group. Each person will be more successful to the extent that he or she can give and accept advice and support. They can all be more successful as each of them develops more insight and skill in leading a team organization.
2. *Point out how they can learn from each other.* Less experienced managers of course learn from the successes and frustrations of more experienced. But more experienced ones learn as they describe their successes and failures and watch others experiment.
3. *Negotiate a contract.* Managers explicitly accept their commitment to help each other become competent team organization leaders. To do this, they agree to attend and participate in the leadership team meetings, to use teamwork as a leadership strategy, and to help others use team organization procedures. This explicit contract is later used as managers reflect on their team.
4. *Offer joint rewards.* The team as a whole is recognized in newsletters, has the opportunity to discuss their group's success with other managers who might be interested in leader teams, attends workshops and courses; each member receives written recommendations that go into their individual files, and each is complemented at performance appraisal for contributions to the team.

Empower

1. *Provide resources.* Managers will need flexibility to schedule convenient meeting times and visit each other's

teams. A small fund for supplies and expenses can facilitate their interaction.

2. *Study the nature of team organization.* Books, lectures, workshops, and discussions help managers deepen their understanding of teamwork.

3. *Structure personal responsibility.* Everyone is expected to contribute, discuss their experiences, observe and give feedback, and be observed and receive feedback. Members take turns providing resources, hosting the meeting, and suppling refreshments.

4. *Show you care.* The leader attends some meetings, serves as an observer, asks for feedback and ideas, and inquires about the progress of the team.

5. *Use "management by walking around" to catch "someone doing something right."* The leader drops in to observe a manager, jots down notes to highlight positive, and gives it to the manager at the next leader development meeting.

Explore

1. *Debate team organization.* Undiscussed doubts and uncertainties undermine team organization. When people discuss their concerns and opposing views, they develop a deeper and more concrete understanding of teamwork.

2. *Create a variety of paths to teamwork.* One manager's approach will not be the same as another. How team organization is applied depends upon the personalities of the players and the opportunities and demands they face.

Reflect

1. *Structure team processing.* The leader helps the team overcome initial reluctance to reflect on its dynamics so that it maintains and develops its relationships. The leader might ask one member to observe and give the team feedback so they can discuss frustrations and conflicts and build upon their successes.

2. *Celebrate successes.* Positive peer recognition is a powerful

incentive that helps managers feel a sense of accomplishment as well as purpose. The leader publicly recognizes concrete examples of progress and has managers swap good news about each other. Peers cheering each other on through quiet recognition and noisy hoopla reinforces the vision and the persistence to overcome obstacles.

Getting Started

Leadership development teams are visible symbols that the leader and managers are sincerely committed to having the organization work as a team. They also are a highly practical way to foster the competence of managers. To capture these benefits, leaders must begin carefully and nurture the teams fully.[3.]

Guides

Leaders should think developmentally, weigh toward success, and build upon small wins. As with team organization more generally, leader teams will experience frustrations and failures, but they should not allowed them to discourage and demoralize them. Leaders structure teams so that they experience successes that they can build upon and celebrate.

Leaders want managers to take a long-term perspective. Managers and their employees do not automatically know how to work together and manage their conflicts. It may take years before people are highly skilled and proficient. The point is to enjoy the progress toward team organization and not be downcast about imperfections. Nurturing and ongoing improvement are their watchwords.

Leaders and managers are committed yet flexible. They remain convinced that they want to work together as a team but are responsive to changes and new directions. They work to integrate, for example, a new emphasis on quality improvement or a strategic initiative to form joint ventures with their commitment to team organization. Team organization is not considered the latest quick fix that will be replaced by next year's fad.

The leader builds him or herself into the group, not out. Do not be the lonely leader on top. The leader is part of the struggle and enjoys the camaraderie, laughter, and sense of purpose and accomplishment of leader development teams.

Steps

1. *Recruit managers for success.* The leader selects the managers who are most interested and skilled in becoming team organization leaders. They ask managers if they are interested, interview them on their understanding of teamwork, and use feedback about how their employees now work together. Managers who like to work together and can meet face-to-face easily can be nominated.

2. *Help structure first meetings.* Managers do not want to sit through more dry, purposeless meetings. The meeting should involve everyone and give them something of value. The leader shows support for their efforts and describes the activities of professional discussions, joint planning, and observation and feedback. The team assesses its resources to make each meeting productive and fun and agrees to a formal or informal contract about their responsibilities. Subsequent meetings include discussion of various aspects of team organization, experiences and concrete problems working as a team, and plans for future work.

3. *Protect and nurture.* The leader communicates that inevitable frustrations, difficulties, and resistance are the "start-up costs" of becoming a team organization. Crises and demands might be setbacks but will not deter the leader and managers from their commitment to put a team organization in place. New innovations will be integrated within team organization.

4. *Back up managers.* Competitive or unknowledgeable managers are apt to criticize managers experimenting with team organization. The leader supports team managers and shows how complaining managers can benefit from learning more about team organization. Union grievances and employee complaints are also handled in a way that supports experimenting managers.

5. *Support the team.* In leader teams, as in other groups,

people will at times hurt, anger, and offend each other. The leader works with the group to manage their conflicts, repair their relationships, and keep them on course.

6. *Be inclusive, not exclusive.* As the first leader group matures, invite others to join. Managers from successful leadership teams can be valuable leaders and members of new groups. Less experienced managers can pair up with more experienced ones in a mentoring relationship.

Team organization challenges managers to transform a collection individuals into a synergistic team. Before this transformation can be complete, managers have to break out of worn-out ideas and habits and change themselves.

Collegial support groups are practical ways for managers to learn from experience. Together managers discuss what they have tried, explore how they can modify their approaches, and deal with inevitable start-up costs and issues. Leader teams are credible signs that the company intends to have a team organization and is committed to the development of managers as leaders and people.

11

Partnership across Organizations

We cannot expect that all nations will adopt like systems, for conformity is the jailer of freedom and the enemy of growth.
—John F. Kennedy, Address to UN General Assembly, 1961

"Singapore?" Lance said to Brian. "Let's get the map out and your bags packed."

"What are we doing there?" Anthony asked.

Brian had just broken the news, which had been rumored for months, that Merchant would be developing an office and hotel complex in Singapore. The boss had explained that the company needed to diversify, and the Asia Pacific was a natural because of its growth and Merchant's location in Seattle. Singapore was considered both prosperous and stable. He also argued, to quiet disbelief, that he had to do the deal secretively because of publicity-shy Asian investors.

Behind the animated teasing, the PMG management team was disappointed, even resentful, that another project was handed to them as a fait accompli. "We could have had a little discussion before we actually committed ourselves," Calvin pointed out.

"I'm disappointed too, and it's a problem for the executive group," Brian said. "I don't want us to spend too much time grumbling. It's an imperfect world, and some things we just have to live with. I want us to focus on what we can do to make this project work for Merchant and PMG."

They brainstormed on possible approaches. Brian announced, "When the going gets tough, I can step in and make the tough decisions. And my decision is advocacy teams."

"I can see the flashbulbs pop and the headlines already: 'Brian

Rescues Merchant from Defeat,'" Janine said to general laughter. "And I can say I know him."

"Now you know why I get paid so much," Brian said. "I've been rethinking things. Maybe there is something to be said for old-fashioned respect for the boss."

"We respect you," Calvin said. "We're just not dazzled by your footwork."

"Janine and Calvin can take the position that we should form a partnership with a local firm for leasing and maintenance and Lance and Anthony that we should set up our own operation there," Brian said. "Do research, find out what others are doing, and be prepared to argue your positions at a meeting ten days from now."

The discussion was lively and spirited and reflected that the groups had read articles, talked to companies that had tried sole ownership and joint ventures, and considered the situation of Merchant. Their consensus decision was to try to form a link with a company in Singapore that knew the local market and conditions. Going it alone would require a greater investment of time and energy and finding a person able and ready to head a local office of PMG.

The discussion made them much more aware of the risks of a cooperative arrangement. Research findings that well over half the joint ventures fail to meet expectations underlined that making their joint venture work would be a challenge. They would have to select a credible company and invest in forging a mutually beneficial arrangement. They would have to bridge the gap between the cultures of the two companies and countries.

"We know working as a team can have great payoffs from our experience, but we also know there are pitfalls to working as a team," Janine summarized.

"Well said," Brian said. "We can put our learning on team organization to work as we form this joint venture. It will be a challenge to apply our framework to working across organizational, cultural, and national boundaries."

Brian and the other managers knew that selecting the right partner was critical; the wrong choice would cost them much time and money. They cast a wide search through notices in business publications and made inquiries about North American companies doing business in Singapore. They asked six viable companies to send information about their company. After debating they arrived at a consensus on three alternatives, sent them detailed information about the project, and requested specific proposals regarding their services and charges.

The proposal also included a statement of the candidate company's philosophy of doing business and the kind of relationship it wanted to establish with Merchant. But the philosophical statements were too similar to be very useful. Singaporeans knew all the right words about participation, cooperation, and teamwork, and while this was reassuring, PMG managers wondered whether these words meant the same to the Singaporeans as it did to them. PMG would have to get behind these generalized, espoused values to get a picture of the actual workings of the company.

Brian and Lance travelled to Singapore to interview the companies on their own turf. They were impressed with the airport and other efficient services and were relieved they could communicate in English. Perhaps this project was a good idea after all.

Good Fortune Properties showed all the signs of being an effective partner. Its present locations were well leased and maintained and had earned good reputations. They were impressed with the company's work ethic, and its people seemed concerned with pleasing Brian and Lance. They decided to select Good Fortune if they could be convinced that they could work as a team with Good Fortune's people.

Writing a vision statement for the project and their partnership was straightforward. They also agreed to a formula by which Good Fortune would get a bonus when leasing and maintenance targets had been reached. Brian and Lance also said that they would explore the possibility that Good Fortune could take a modest equity position in the complex and share in any equity growth. Brian, Lance, and Good Fortune's representatives worked out arrangements for communicating between personnel in Singapore and Seattle so that they could keep each other informed. Face-to-face meetings would at first occur semiannually.

The more difficult part was communicating that PMG wanted to discuss problems and different views open-mindedly and to reflect on relationship issues and manage conflicts constructively. Brian and Lance gave examples, discussed the ideas of constructive controversy and positive conflict management, and emphasized their hope and expectations that the joint venture would work along these principles. It was not that the Singaporeans disagreed, but it was not clear that they fully understood and accepted this approach.

The two sides agreed to take turns visiting each other's offices and discussing issues and problems. Brian and Lance realized that they would have to take the initiative by asking their colleagues to voice their concerns and then open-mindedly responding to them.

On the plane ride home, Brian and Lance reflected on their progress. They were pleased that they could recommend Good Fortune and had a tentative agreement. They also knew that they would have to invest in their relationship with the Singaporeans.

"I think we'll have fun getting to know these Singaporeans," Brian said. "You know, the buildings and so much of the country looks like a North American city, but I think we learned enough to know that such appearances mask real differences in how we manage and work together. We'll probably learn a lot."

"We'll need that kind of attitude and lots of patience to be successful," Lance said. "We can't just drive in and get the job done fast. We must take the time to understand them as people and appreciate their way of thinking and working. Otherwise I can see us getting very frustrated and the relationship falling apart."

Global Competition and Cooperative Ventures

Merchant and many other firms recognize that the global marketplace has made it easier for competitors to penetrate their home markets. But the global market also opens up new markets and new ways of doing business. To take advantage of these possibilities firms are forming cooperative links with companies in other countries. The international marketplace creates both more competition and more opportunities for cooperation.

Joint ventures and other cooperative agreements are becoming the major vehicles for international business. It has been estimated that U.S. firms rely on them four times more than fully owned subsidiaries.[1] Whereas U.S. firms own ten thousand foreign subsidiaries fully, they share ownership in another fifteen thousand and have thirty thousand overseas agreements with little or no equity stake. Many foreign business people are looking for U.S. partners to enter the American market. Cooperative arrangements are even more popular for European and Japanese firms.

Cooperative ventures have many advantages.[2] They allow for expansion yet reduce risks for any one firm. Combined resources and technology exchange make the venture stronger than independent action. A local company may have the marketing contacts and savvy necessary to succeed in that country; the foreign-based one has access to technology and favorably priced capital. Agreements limit costly competition because potential competitors agree to work together. Joint ventures also meet government concerns and barriers against foreign ownership. Cooperative ventures are widely thought to be major ways to stimulate genuine global prosperity and recognition of mutual interdependence.

Cooperative arrangements are an important, practical tool. General Electric, for example, has ten thousand products and cannot invest in all of them. It has scores of foreign affiliates, several hundred licensing and production contracts, and minority joint ventures to manufacture and market its products worldwide.

Risks and Pitfalls

Joint ventures, especially international ones, have potentially high risks as well as high yields. A company may use access to its partner's technology to become a competitor.[3] Demands to communicate and negotiate agreements require a great deal of top management's attention and distract them from other opportunities. Though popular, international joint ventures have a high failure rate.[4]

Joint ventures pose difficult management challenges.[5] They typically involve diverse workforces that must try to work together.

(See Dean Tjosvold's *Team Organization* for more information on managing diversity within a firm.) Parent firms may disagree about staffing patterns, in particular whose employees will hold the most important positions. Local managers may feel their potential for future promotions is blocked; whereas employees from the foreign parent may worry that their promotion opportunities are limited back at the home office. Employees may have split loyalty and be caught in dilemmas about what parent company to support. The different compensation practices of the two companies may create friction and a sense of inequity. Geographical distance and cultural barriers interfere with communication exchange.

Cooperative partnerships often do not have the credible, consistent management needed to deal with the complex, tough issues and conflicts they create. Teamwork is difficult to create within one company, but international joint ventures require collaboration across nations, cultures, and vast geographical distances.

In addition to imposing obstacles, the new venture has not had time to evolve and establish operating methods. A new organization must be forged out of two already established companies. In most companies, the accepted values and ways of working are implicit and cannot be communicated very directly and fully. When inevitably people fail to live up to the implicit expectations of the other company, they are unsure what to do because they do not know each other well and have not established procedures for conflict management.

Structuring Cooperative Arrangements

The team organization model provides a common framework for collaboration across organizations. People from different companies explicitly agree on how they are to work together and develop common expectations and adequate procedures. Once frustrations and difficulties occur, they are more confident that they have the wherewithal to manage them constructively.

Networking between organizations draws upon many of the same steps as creating the team organization within a company using the parts of the model:

ENVISION

1. In addition to establishing the business, partners focus specifically on the kind of relationships they want. The team organization provides a framework upon which they can build.

2. Partners demonstrate their commitment to working as a team as they negotiate the joint venture.

UNITE

1. Tangible cooperative rewards back up general principles of mutual benefit. Both sides see clearly how they will benefit from joint success.

2. Partners recognize and respond to each side's particular interests and requirements. They discuss opposing interests directly and work out compromises.

EMPOWER

1. Partners show they want to learn about each other and from each other. They discuss how the principles of teamwork apply in their cultures and how diverse people have different ways of indicating they want to work as a cooperative team.

2. Partners take seminars and workshops on teamwork and conflict management and discuss how they can apply their learning to the cooperative venture.

EXPLORE

1. Partners discuss and create procedures that are acceptable and functional for all. Working across organizational, cultural, and national boundaries requires a creative use of telephones, fax machines, and computer lines.

2. No one side assumes its procedures are superior and tries to impose them on the other.

REFLECT

1. Partners commit themselves to regular reviews of progress on business and team organization. They discuss problems before they become crises.

2. Partners respect the traditional ways that people in different cultures and organizations have learned to manage conflict.

Creating Unity: A General Motors and Toyota Joint Venture

When I try to set up joint ventures, for example, a medical imaging center involving the hospital, physicians, and private investors, the only way to make it work is to demonstrate to each party what they have to gain. And how what they have to gain can only happen if they work together.

—Bob Phillips, President, Health Business Development Associates

Joint ventures underline the importance, and difficulty, of forging unity. There is no common membership or sense of community to serve as a powerful indicator of cooperative goals. Many joint ventures cross national boundaries and add the complexities of cross-cultural communication.

General Motors and Toyota, fierce competitors in the automobile market, still understood that in some areas cooperation could be highly useful. After preliminary discussions, executives from both companies met in March 1982, and announced plans for a joint venture, New United Motor Manufacturing Inc. (NUMMI). The venture would produce a new subcompact at GM's old Fremont, California, plant for the U.S. market.

Both companies formed the joint venture for significant self-interests. GM wanted to replace its subcompact, the Chevette, to respond to competition in that market niche. The corporation needed a new model that would meet its fuel standards for the cars sold in the United States, and it wanted to improve relations with UAW by employing laid-off workers. GM thought that it could use a model Toyota had already developed for the Japanese market. Toyota's production methods gave them a $1,500 to $2,000 advantage per car, and GM wanted to how to put those methods to work here. Such improvements would help win back customers to GM products.

Toyota, too, saw significant gains in such a plan. Both the Japanese and U.S. governments were pressing Toyota to establish U.S. production so as to reduce the U.S. trade deficit with Japan. Toyota had reservations about U.S. production and had let Honda and Nissan take the lead. But a joint venture would reduce the costs of determining the feasibility of U.S. production. GM would also give Toyota access to the world's most extensive supplier of automobile parts.

In addition to developing a consensus within each company, participants had to go through arduous, complex negotiating to realize these significant advantages. In April 1982, teams from each company met and were assigned such issues as facilities planning, costing, planning, and labor to different working groups. They set September as the target to reach a final agreement.

Though each side was thoroughly prepared, the negotiations were much more complex than anticipated. There were, for example, a great number of parts and the two companies had to make decisions about who was to make them. They each had different styles of negotiating. The Americans liked to get down to specific proposals quickly; whereas the Japanese wanted to discuss broad issues first. The Americans thought that the Japanese were too indirect and often interpreted silence as meaning agreement. The Americans could access information from their organizations more quickly than the Japanese.

Five months after their deadline, on February 14, 1983, the companies announced that they had reached a final agreement that would save capital and share risks. Toyota had eased government pressures and also had a foothold for competing against Nissan and Honda on U.S.-made cars, but at half the cost. GM had a new subcompact at billions of dollars less than if it designed the car itself. Producing quality cars and learning from each other would make the joint venture pay off, but GM and Toyota would have to continue to negotiate and emphasize their cooperative goals to make this joint venture work.

Linking Buyers and Suppliers: General Motors and Velcro

Companies have been reminded that listening to customers is critical for survival. It is only through satisfying customers that companies receive necessary support and resources. But listening to customers is just the first step. An organization must show that customers are vital to its vision and that it is committed to their welfare: it has open lines of communication, explores customer problems, and keeps in touch with them.

Velcro had to learn to form a new partnership with GM in order to keep GM as a customer. GM was working with suppliers to improve the quality of their products and the reliability of their deliveries. Because suppliers add over half the cost of an automobile, GM and other manufacturers have recognized that their success depends upon having successful suppliers, so they have instituted programs to get the suppliers involved in quality programs.

One morning in August 1985, a General Motors sales manager informed Velcro that it had dropped from its highest supplier quality rating to its fourth.[6] Velcro would have ninety days to begin a program of total quality control or face the prospect of losing an important customer. GM was dissatisfied that Velcro was not building quality into the product, was throwing away from 5 percent to 8 percent of the tape and passing the costs on to GM. GM made it clear that Velcro had to be organized around ongoing improvement.

Velcro used those ninety days to orient employees, establish improvement teams, and set up a steering committee to monitor the progress of the teams. Having the president and the heads of sales, finance, personnel, marketing, manufacturing, R&D, quality, and information systems on the steering committee clearly signalled that quality was a priority. GM agreed that Velcro was on the right track and would check up again in six months.

The first ninety days were just the beginning. Velcro had to involve everybody from the top down to show them how quality was vital to the survival of the company; the message from GM made that message credible. The steering committee met regularly every two weeks to hear progress reports from continuous improvement teams. The president also modeled the way by being a member of one of the quality improvement teams. The company's newsletter usually had a lead article about quality by an improvement team. Employee teams trained operators, repaired and redesigned machinery, and measured and reported quality results. Teams also focused on the organization to improve up-and-down communication, accuracy of payroll, and to reduce paperwork. Indeed, about half of the fifty teams operating at any one time worked on administrative issues.

The quality program paid off. Velcro reduced waste as a percentage of total manufacturing expense by 50 percent in 1987 from 1986, and another 45 percent in 1988 from 1987. GM recognized Velcro's success by improving its quality rating. However, Velcro must continue to drive for quality because GM and other auto makers keep raising standards and expectations.

Teamwork spills out across organizations. Companies are finding, as individuals have, that they cannot run a business all by themselves. They work with suppliers to improve quality, use community resources to develop a business, and form joint ventures to take advantage of opportunities. Industry associations promote a business climate and lobby government for favorable legislation and rulings. Companies assist with community services, environmental groups, and schools to promote the quality of life of their employees and the development of future employees. Organizations depend on their environment and need teamwork to respond and influence it.

The team organization provides a common framework to forge partnerships. One company cannot simply transport and impose its procedures and operations on the other. The opportunity is liberating because people are able to explore and to create more productive, humane ways of working. Unfortunately, the stereotypes and confusions that people have about leadership and teamwork lead to frustrating procedures. To use the freedom to create a new organization requires knowledge of productive teamwork.

12

Developing Your Team Organization

The greatest improvement in the productive powers of labor, and the greater part of the skill, dexterity, and judgment with which it is anywhere directed or applied, seem to have been the effect of the division of labor.

—Adam Smith, Wealth of Nations

We are going to win and the industrial West is going to lose out: there's nothing much you can do about it, because the reasons for failure are within yourself . . . for you the essence of management is getting the ideas out of the heads of the bosses into the hand of labor. . . . for us, the core of management is precisely the act of mobilizing and pulling together the intellectual resources of all employees . . . only by drawing on the combined brainpower of all its employees can a firm face up to the turbulence and constraints of today's environment.

—Konosuke Matsushita, Executive Director, Matsushita Electric

"I think I enjoyed that debate as much as you did," Janine said to Brian. They had just listened to the task force present and defend its recommendations on revamping the compensation system at PMG. Task force members and Anthony and Calvin had already left; Janine, Brian, and Lance were walking out the door.

"Really good," Brian said. "As I said to the task force, why would anyone want to manage a company any other way?"

"But Brian, don't you mind that we didn't make a decision, that they have to refine their proposal, and then we have to bring it to all the managers?" Lance asked. "It takes a lot of time. Sometimes I think we could do it much more efficiently ourselves."

"I'm not sure that we would have thought about all the issues and developed such a package," Janine said. "We would have been much more doctrinaire. We want a team reward, so here it is. This team wants us to think seriously about what fairness means, ways to make incentives meaningful, and how we can deal with those not doing their fair share."

"Wasn't that exciting to see them get into the issues and together hammer out a solution," Brian observed. "They take philosophical issues of fairness and unity seriously, but they are also very practical. I agree we would be more ideological, more simple-minded."

"But we don't necessarily want complex solutions," Lance pointed out.

"I like elegant solutions, too, but our important problems don't have simple-minded solutions," Brian said. "The involvement and debate we had today helps us put together a plan that considers many viewpoints. The result should be practical and elegant, not complex and obscure."

"And you have to admit, it was fun," Janine said.

"I like to mix it up," Lance said.

"Me too," Brian said. "I enjoyed watching them mix it up. I admit to a gnawing feeling that somehow I should be working harder at these meetings, especially one on compensation! It's like I should be proving that I'm the boss and deserve my salary. But I'm getting better at suppressing such feelings."

"The process is fine. I worry about the outcomes," Lance said.

"We'll have to measure the impact of the compensation plan," Brian said. "There is no guarantee that all this discussion will lead to a plan that will work well. But what I don't have to wait to find out is that people are really involved and discussing different positions together and constructively. That kind of process is the essence of what we are trying to do, and we can direct that effort to serving our customers, dealing with problems, finding new services, you name it. Once we get everyone doing this, the potential of it all just staggers me. It will be beauty and power in action."

"I'm glad you're feeling good about the division," Janine said. "I'm more confident about myself as a manager and a leader. I find our employees more supportive and open."

"There are better feelings around the place, if that means anything," Lance added.

"It does," Brian said. "Feeling sullen, stressed, or upset just does not cut it. How can you be productive, innovative, and all those other good things in the long run if you're not enjoying yourself and your colleagues? Life's too short to live that way."

"Speaking of short, I didn't realize it's nearly five o'clock," Lance said. "I've some more things to do before I go home tonight."

"You all can stay, but I'm going home," Brian said. "I want to say hello to my family before my daughter and I run off to basketball practice."

"You're still enjoying coaching?" Janine asked.

"Great time," Brian said. "The shooting, dribbling, everything is new to these girls, and they're so eager to learn. They're not into the posturing, grandstanding, and blaming that you get with some jaded kids. They know there's much more to playing basketball than who puts the basketball into the hoop."

"Team organization on the girls' basketball court," Lance said.

"Sure, I tell them over and over that to be successful and enjoy basketball means they have to pass, set up plays, and pull together," Brian said. "They understand. The parents need some convincing about why I give all the girls playing time. I gave the noisiest father some articles on teamwork."

"Bet he loved that," Lance said.

"To his credit, he read them and said he had a better understanding of where I'm coming from," Brian said. "His daughter is having such a good experience that he's rethinking his attitude a bit."

The personal, warm conversation with Janine and Lance had gotten Brian into a reflective mood as he drove home. He couldn't quite put his finger on it, but he felt both contented and energized. It was not that he was completely satisfied. There were challenges and problems at home and work that needed attention. He had to be disciplined and watchful as he continued to build his relationship with his son and with his boss and peers.

The phrase that seemed to capture his feelings was "coming together." The family and division were coming together, and so was he. He felt whole and complete and free. He had direction and purpose, but he could still change. He supported people and made demands on them; he expressed his love and his anger. He consistently sought team relationships but acted flexibly. Perhaps most liberating was that he was both himself and a leader. He was known and accepted by his colleagues and employees, just as he knew and accepted them. He was grateful for his good fortune.

Principles of Change

Managers and employees at PMG and other companies have to continue to invest in their team organization or risk stagnation and fragmentation. Becoming a team organization requires continuous improvement but has ongoing payoffs.

Genuine relationships, respect for all, and give-and-take are basic human values upon which team organization builds. Yet putting these fundamental values into place in our organizations has been elusive. Posturing, self-protection, and conformity are often seen as a more realistic description of how our organizations work, and these modes are defended as necessary for organizations to survive and prosper in a competitive business environment.

Teamwork is needed to create the team organization. The team organization model outlines ideals leaders and followers should strive for and suggests how they can be accomplished. The model is both the end and the means. Employees work in teams to learn and apply the model to their organization. These teams have a vision and cooperative unity to strengthen their organization. They dig into issues, explore alternative points of view, and solve problems. They recognize that creating a team organization is an ongoing process, not a one-shot affair. The methods to create the team organization reinforce the message.

As they apply the model to themselves, people gain a deeper understanding of what it takes to be an effective team. Team members collect valid, useful data through questionnaire surveys, interviews, and observations to identify their strengths and weaknesses. They put this understanding to work by developing plans to improve their team. They are strengthening their team as they learn to analyze and lead teams.

Employees work simultaneously on developing themselves as a unified force as well as dealing with business issues. They use their team understanding and skills to explore important problems and make specific operational business decisions.

Steps for Change

Leaders and followers learn and apply the team organization model to make their organization into a flexible, united force. They have the shared vision of a team organization, feel they are united behind this vision, work together to develop the common understanding and skills of effective teamwork, use their various ideas to create facilitative, appropriate procedures and ways of working, and continually extend and strengthen cooperative teamwork throughout the organization.

Envision

Managers and employees first get exposure to the model and gain a sense of its power and usefulness. Reading this and other books and articles, getting involved in discussions about teamwork, attending seminars and presentations, and talking to people already using teamwork and the team model help people explore issues further. Perhaps the most convincing evidence is the experience of using the model.

Unite

The payoff of the team organization is real and substantial. The company and employees benefit from improved productivity and innovation, challenges, and support, and personal confidence and self-awareness. Our knowledge has exposed the myths that a company must choose between being productive or being people-oriented, that what is good for management hurts employees.

Empower

Leaders and followers are on the same wavelength in their commitment to strengthening the team and have a shared set of aspirations for it. In addition to describing the business mission, leaders convey their commitment to the vision that people will work as a team. Employees ask questions, emphasize certain points, and fill out the meaning teamwork has for them. Managers and employees together study the nature of team organization and create workshops, task forces, and other forums so that they can discuss how to apply team organization principles.

Explore

The team decides and takes joint action to be an effective team. Managers and employees debate recommendations to strengthen the team's vision, to feel more united, to be more empowered, to explore issues thoroughly, and to reflect for continuous improvement. They work to achieve a living, workable consensus on the company's direction. They structure job assignments, rewards, and norms to strengthen unity. They refine communication and productive conflict skills to feel empowered.

Reflect

Recognizing the need to continue to invest in their groups and organizations or risk creating suspicions and unresolved hostilities, team members commit themselves to dealing with conflicts directly and openly. They schedule regular sessions to reflect on how they are working together. They celebrate successes and use their learning to strive for ongoing improvement. Managers form leader development teams to discuss ideas, make plans, jointly overcome barriers, and celebrate successes as they create cooperative teams.

Formulating a Team Organization Program

Deciding how to begin creating a team organization should, like other important issues, be discussed and debated. In a leader development team or other group leaders can use the following questions as a guide to planning how to begin a team organization program.

Envision. How can you help people see the value of working as a team? How can the value of teamwork be demonstrated and skepticism be dealt with directly?

Unite. What will help people see that team organization pays off for all and unites them in a vital, common effort? What

experiences can help people identify their important interests
and see how they overlap with others'?

Empower. How can you help people understand the team
organization model? What are the confusions that will get in
their way? What are critical first steps that will clarify what
team organization is and show that they can accomplish it?

Explore. How can you help people work together to forge a
team organization? What are the forums most conducive to
productive collaboration? What aspects of the structure,
rewards, training and other programs can be changed? What
aspects cannot be changed and must be lived with?

Reflect. How can the attitude and practices of ongoing
experimenting and improvement in how people work
together be developed? What forums and procedures will
facilitate feedback and discussion about relationships and
conflicts?

Meeting Challenges

The hottest places in Hell are reserved for those who, in a time of great
moral crisis, maintain their neutrality.

—Dante

Leadership for teamwork addresses the most fundamental obstacle
to strengthening our business, public, educational, and family organizations. We need collective effort to confront the suspicion and
barriers that divide us so that we can be prepared to work together.
Then we have the potential power to regain marketshare, improve
the quality of products and services, support the family, and revitalize our schools.

Team organization questions some contemporary myths: the
ideal of "the rugged individualist," the leader as charismatic hero,
and the idea that competition has made the capitalist countries successful. Teamwork is essential to our lives and built into our spe-
cies. We want to be part of something larger than ourselves, be
respected and connected to others, and feel invigorated and accepted by them. Only then can we accomplish the extraordinary and
develop ourselves as people and leaders.

Though we can capture our traditional teamwork, we cannot replicate craft organizations or village life. We are not going to work and live as our grandparents, or even as our parents did. The team organization model summarizes current knowledge to help us experiment and forge our own organizations. With these tools we can exercise our freedom to create synergistic teamwork to confront our common predicaments and fulfill our common aspirations.

Appendix

Guides for Action and Pitfalls to Avoid
—An Action Summary

Chapter 2: Confronting Leadership

Guides for Action

- Admit to feelings of fear as well as excitement at becoming a leader.
- Discuss your leadership concerns with knowledgeable friends.
- Open-mindedly consider new approaches to leading.
- Recognize leaders as architects of teamwork.
- Appreciate the value of investing in relationships.
- Take the long-term view.
- Develop a support group to help you challenge the status quo.
- Describe the costs of a competitive-independent climate and the value of spirited, meaningful cooperative teamwork.
- Show people how teamwork brings them together.
- Plan how you can make a difference helping others make a difference.

Pitfalls to Avoid

- Assume your success means you can stop learning.
- Ignore concerns and fears about being a leader.
- Try to be a leader by yourself.
- Redouble your efforts when you feel ineffective to avoid reflecting on your leadership approach.
- Concentrate first on getting tasks completed.
- Show an urgency only for the short-term.

- Wait for a crisis before dealing with relationships.
- Assume competition is naturally healthy.
- Be complacent by arguing that competition is inevitable.
- Let someone else take the risk of changing the system.

Chapter 3: Fostering Team Leader Relationships

Guides for Action

- Invest in your relationships continually.
- Be consistent in your intent to form cooperative relationships with employees; be flexible in your actions.
- Respect employees as people.
- Trust employees so that they trust you.
- Cheer employees on and encourage their heart.
- Ask and use the ideas and assistance of employees.
- Be open to influence as you expect others to be open to yours.
- Express genuine warmth and caring for employees.
- Recognize employees and their achievements as reflecting their personal strengths.

Pitfalls to Avoid

- Believe you can lead by yourself.
- Assume leadership is for the few.
- Search for one right plan of action good for all situations and people.
- Have no commitments other than to do what the situation calls for.
- Prove you are always right.
- Blame someone for every problem.
- Keep an interpersonal distance from employees.
- Assume money is enough of a reward for employees.
- Conclude that feeling overworked and stressed means you are doing your job.
- Try to make yourself indispensible by not sharing information.

Chapter 3: Managing Your Boss

- Recognize the need to work with your boss.
- Appreciate the pressures and problems your boss faces.
- Understand her goals and how you can further them.
- Inform her of your aspirations and interests.
- Identify how she likes to work with employees.
- Make her working with you efficient and enjoyable.
- Keep her posted on your successes and difficulties.
- Make it easy for her to bring up problems and conflicts.
- Show you appreciate her effort and support.

Pitfalls to Avoid

- Believe your boss's job is much easier than your own.
- Assume your boss knows your goals and problems.
- Assume you know your boss's goals and problems.
- Talk to him only when he asks.
- Assume he will initiate a discussion if he is concerned with your performance.
- Believe he gets paid so well he does not need your thanks.
- Only tell him of your successes and cover up your failures.

Chapter 5: Approaching Your Team

Guides for Action

- Express your commitment to team organization.
- Provide background reading and material.
- Structure discussion and debate.
- Open-mindedly explore limitations of your model of teamwork.
- Admit when you and your team fall short of the ideal.
- Reflect on specific strengths and weaknesses of the team.
- Allow people the time and opportunity to explore and change.
- Make the method consistent with the message.
- Work with the team as it discusses teamwork.
- Express your conviction that the team can strengthen itself.

- Build yourself in as a team member.

Pitfalls to Avoid

- Insist on quick agreement and action.
- Assume everyone has to agree with you.
- Take all criticisms as narrow-minded resistance.
- Take all doubt as disinterest.
- Assume no one agrees with you.
- Build yourself out of the team as a consultant.

Chapter 6: Reaching Out to Managers and Supervisors

Guides for Action

- Make a personal, vigorous statement of your conviction to teamwork.
- Use jigsaw to help people understand team organization.
- Structure discussion to deepen understanding.
- Form small discussion groups (three to six people) out of a large one.
- Assign people who don't know each other to a group and in other ways encourage relationships and communication.
- Foster critique of the model.
- Build momentum yet allow time for full debate.
- Encourage people from all ranks to speak their minds.
- Work for a common understanding and strategic direction.
- Identify ways that the group as a whole can work together.
- Plan how to use task forces and other forums to explore specific issues and make recommendations.
- Use ad hoc decision making to review and revise recommendations.

Pitfalls to Avoid

- Assume everyone has the same definition of teamwork.
- Keep knowledge about team organization to yourself.
- Assume everyone must sit around one table.
- Worry only about what is to be discussed, not how.

- Dominate the discussion.
- Assume people will discuss if they care enough.
- Discuss specific issues in a large group.
- Make decisions on complex problems without prior consideration by a small problem-solving team.

Chapter 7: Including the Union

Guides for Action

- Respect the union's legitimacy.
- Know why working with union leaders will pay off for you, them, and employees.
- Work for a cooperative relationship with the union.
- Take the first, second, and third steps in approaching the union.
- Respect the style of union leaders.
- Appreciate that union leaders must respond to their constituency.
- Listen to union leaders ventilate.
- Paraphrase and show you understand union concerns.
- Argue that unions can help people speak out on issues, protect the right to dissent, and correct injustices and grievances.
- Keep up the momentum to build a team organization while allowing people time to adjust and change their attitudes.

Pitfalls to Avoid

- Assume the union leadership is the enemy.
- Blame all problems on the union.
- Be ready to retaliate every blow and slight.
- Assume you must prove you are as tough and can talk as hard as any union leader.
- Assert your authority over the union.
- Assume because the union leadership is competitive, you must be too.
- Imply that union leaders will have to smooth over their conflicts with the company.

- Equate convincing a union leader with convincing the union membership and workforce.
- Allow yourself to get distracted from building a team organization.

Chapter 8: Forming a Cohesive Department

Guides for Action

- Discuss how team organization can make department members feel supported as people and effective as employees.
- Detail how working on developing team organization will pay off for customers.
- Use questionnaires and interviews to collect feedback on the department's customers.
- Have customers talk face-to-face with the department.
- Reflect on feedback from customers.
- Use questionnaires and interviews to collect feedback on relationships within the department.
- Have the team draw a picture or an image of itself.
- Reflect on the strengths and frustrations of the department as a team.
- Identify and begin to deal with specific barriers and aids to the team effort.

Pitfalls to Avoid

- Dismiss feedback from customers as unrealistic grumbling.
- Accept as inevitable the department's shortcomings.
- Assume that having people work in isolation is good enough.
- Assume that if people are willing to help when asked that is all that is required to be a team.
- Demand more resources as the solution to every problem.

Chapter 8: Forming Employee Teams

Guides for Action

- Speak directly about your desire to work together with employees.

- Define employee jobs broadly to include working together to improve the quality of work life and company effectiveness.
- Share information so that employees are aware of the successes, obligations, and obstacles the business faces.
- Defend the need to make a return on investment and give returns to stakeholders.
- Consider workers valuable allies to enhance service quality and create value-added products.
- Confront the assumed trade-off between company and employee welfare.
- Develop appropriate procedures and skills for employee teams.
- Help employees learn to manage their conflicts and develop their relationships.

Pitfalls to Avoid

- Expect employees to care when they have little information about the company's pressures.
- Expect supervisors by themselves to gain employee cooperation.
- Assume the solution is to lower labor costs.
- Blame management for shortcomings.
- Blame workers for shortcomings.
- Accept "win-lose" attitudes between management and employees as inevitable.
- Assume that allowing employee teams to be self-managing is enough to make them effective.

Chapter 9: Using Constructive Controversy

Guides for Action

- Elaborate positions and ideas.
- List facts, information, and theories.
- Ask for clarification.
- Clarify opposing ideas.
- Challenge opposing ideas and positions.
- Reaffirm your confidence in those who differ.
- Identify strengths in opposing arguments.

- Search for new information.
- Integrate various information and reasoning.
- Create a solution responsive to several points of view.

Pitfalls to Avoid

- Assume your position is superior.
- Prove your ideas are "right" and must be accepted.
- Interpret opposition to your ideas as a personal attack.
- Refuse to admit weaknesses in your position.
- Pretend to listen.

Chapter 9: Facilitating Problem-Solving Teams

Guides for Action

- Assign an important, challenging, and concrete problem.
- Include people with independent, diverse views and backgrounds.
- Discuss problems so that all team members understand the value of constructive controversy.
- Practice constructive controversy to improve skills and confidence.
- Use advocacy teams to structure constructive controversy.
- Provide needed time and resources to explore the problem in depth.
- Evaluate alternatives for their tangible and intangible consequences for the team, the company, and other stakeholders.
- Use consensus decision making.
- Debate the team's recommendation until people inside and outside the team are committed to a solution.
- Make a responsibility chart that outlines who is responsible for what when.
- Evaluate the process of implementation.
- Evaluate the impact of the implemented solution.
- Celebrate achievements and the feeling of being in charge of problems, not controlled by them.
- Identify new problems to tackle and solve.

Pitfalls to Avoid

- Assign minor issues to the team, and keep the important ones for yourself.
- Insist on solutions now.
- Encourage people to become totally committed to their own position.
- Don't worry about the problem, just the solution.
- Commit to the first reasonable idea as the solution.
- Reject ideas because they come from unexpected sources.
- Dismiss ideas that cannot be quickly justified.
- Argue that majority voting is the only democratic way.
- Accept or reject the recommendations of a task force without discussion and debate.
- Assume once a solution is agreed upon, the problem is gone.
- Assume once a solution is implemented, the problem is taken care of.
- Expect clear sailing with no problems.

Chapter 10: Structuring Leader Development Teams

Guides for Action

- Show how leader teams fit into team organization.
- Specify how leader teams help managers as professionals and people.
- Identify the activities of leader teams.
- Work with the teams to help them be effective.
- Learn from mistakes as well as successes.
- Build on the success of the first team.
- Include as many managers as volunteer.

Pitfalls to Avoid

- Let managers fend for themselves.
- Assume that getting managers together means they will support each other's learning.
- Believe only young persons can learn.

Chapter 11: Structuring Partnerships

Guides for Action

- Communicate your intent to work as a team.
- Suggest team organization as a common ideal and model.
- Negotiate consistent with team principles.
- Identify how the partnership is mutually beneficial.
- Respond to the interests and concerns of the partner.
- Appreciate each other's styles and procedures.
- Study and develop teamwork procedures together.
- Structure regular sessions to solve problems before they become crises.
- Be firm about the need to manage conflicts; be flexible about how they are managed.

Pitfalls to Avoid

- Focus only on the business vision and arrangements, and ignore the organization.
- Believe you and the other company have similar ways of working.
- Assume your organizational methods are superior.
- Impose your way of working.

Notes

Preface

1. Zemke, R., & D. Schaff. (1989). *The service edge: 101 companies that profit from customer care.* (New York: New American Library), 5.
2. Seligman, Martin E. P. (1988). Boomer blues. *Psychology Today,* October, 50–55.
3. *Statistics Canada Yearbook 1990* (1990). Ottawa: John Dyell Company.
4. Ibid.
5. Farnham, A. (1989). The trust gap. *Fortune,* 4 December, 56–78.

Chapter 1

1. Deutsch, M. (1990). Sixty years of conflict. *International Journal of Conflict Management* 1: 237–63; Deutsch, M. (1985). *Distributive justice: A social-psychological perspective.* New Haven, Conn.: Yale University Press; Deutsch, M. (1980). Fifty years of conflict. In *Retrospections on social psychology,* ed. L. Festinger. New York: Oxford University Press, 46–77; Deutsch, M. (1973). *The resolution of conflict.* New Haven, Conn.: Yale University Press; Johnson, D.W., & R. T. Johnson. (1989). *Cooperation and competition: Theory and research.* Edina, Minn.: Interaction Book Company; Johnson, D.W., G. Maruyama, R.T. Johnson, D. Nelson, & S. Skon. (1981). Effect of cooperative, competitive, and individualistic goal structures on achievement: A meta-analysis. *Psychological Bulletin* 89: 47–62; Tjosvold, D. (1991). *Team organization: An enduring competitive advantage.* New York: Wiley; Tjosvold, D. (1986). *Working together to get things done: Managing for organizational productivity.* Lexington, Mass.: D.C. Heath.
2. Kouzes, J.M., & B.Z. Posner. (1987). *The leadership challenge.* San Francisco: Jossey-Bass.

Chapter 3

1. Helmreich. R. (1982). *Pilot selection and training.* Paper presented at the an-

nual meeting of the American Psychological Association, August, Washington, D.C.: Helmreich; Beane, R., W. Lucker, & J. Spence. (1978). Achievement motivation and scientific attainment. *Personality and Social Psychological Bulletin* 4: 222–26. Helmreich, R., L. Sawin, & A. Carsrud. (1986). The honeymoon effect in job performance: Temporal increases in the predictive power of achievement motivation. *Journal of Applied Psychology* 71: 185–88; Helmreich, R. Spence, J. Beane, W. Lucker, & K. Matthews. (1980). Making it in academic psychology: Demographic and personality correlates of attainment. *Journal of Personality and Social Psychology* 39: 896–908.

2. Tjosvold, D., I. R. Andrews, & H. Jones. (1983). Cooperative and competitive relationships between leaders and their subordinates. *Human Relations* 36: 1111–24.

3. Tjosvold, D. (1988). Interdependence and power between managers and employees: A study of the leader relationship. *Journal of Management* 15: 49–64.

4. Kanter, R. M. (1979). Power failure in management circuits. *Harvard Business Review*, July-August 65–75; Kanter, R. M. (1977). *Men and women of the corporation.* New York: Basic Books. (in press).

5. Tjosvold, D., I. R. Andrews, & J. Struthers. (in press). Power and interdependence in work groups: Views of managers and employees. *Group & Organization Studies;* Tjosvold, D. (1990). Power in cooperative and competitive organizational contexts. *Journal of Social Psychology* 130: 249–58; Tjosvold, D. (1985). The effects of attribution and social context on superiors' influence and interaction with low performing subordinates. *Personnel Psychology* 38: 361–76; Tjosvold, D. (1985). Power and social context in superior-subordinate interaction. *Organizational Behavior and Human Decision Processes* 35: 281–93; Tjosvold, D. (1981). Unequal power relationships within a cooperative or competitive context, *Journal of Applied Social Psychology* 11: 137–50.

6. Tjosvold, D. (1990). Cooperation and competition in restructuring an organization. *Canadian Journal of Administrative Sciences* 7: 48–54; Tjosvold, D. (1990). Flight crew coordination to manage safety risks. *Group & Organization Studies* 15: 177–91; Tjosvold, D. (1990). Making a technological innovation work: Collaboration to solve problems. *Human Relations* 43: 1117–31; Tjosvold, D. (1990). Power in cooperative and competitive organizational contexts. *Journal of Social Psychology* 130: 249–58; Tjosvold, D. (1988). Cooperative and competitive interdependence: Collaboration between departments to serve customers. *Group & Organization Studies* 13: 274–89; Tjosvold, D. (1988). Interdependence and power between managers and employees: A study of the leader relationship. *Journal of Management* 15: 49–64.

7. Tjosvold, D., I. R. Andrews, & H. Jones. (1985). Alternative ways leaders can use authority. *Canadian Journal of Administrative Sciences* 2; 307–17.

8. Richter, F., & D. Tjosvold. (1981). Effects of student participation in classroom decision-making on attitudes, peer interaction, motivation, and learning. *Journal of Applied Psychology* 65: 74–80; Tjosvold, D. (1991). Achieving productive synergy by integrating departmental efforts. In *Applying psychology in business: The manager's handbook,* ed. J. W. Jones, B. D. Steffy, and D. W.

Bray. (1991), Lexington, Mass.: D. C. Heath, 595–601; Tjosvold, D. (1987). Participation: A close look at its dynamics. *Journal of Management* 13: 739–50; Tjosvold, D. (1985). Dynamics within participation: An experimental investigation. *Group & Organizational Studies* 10: 260–77.

9. Tjosvold, D., I. R. Andrews, & J. Struthers. (in press). Leadership influence: Goal interdependence and power. *Journal of Social Psychology;* Tjosvold, D., D. W. Johnson, & R. T. Johnson. (1984). Influence strategy, perspective-taking, and relationships between high and low power individuals in cooperative and competitive contexts. *Journal of Psychology* 116: 187–202.

10. Ellis, R. J. (1988). Self-monitoring and leadership emergence in groups. *Personality and Social Psychology Bulletin* 14: 681–93; McClelland, D. C., & R. E. Boyatzis. Leadership motive pattern and long-term success in management. *Journal of Applied Psychology* 67: 737–43; Johnson, D. W. & R. T. Johnson. (1989). *Leading the cooperative school.* Edina, Minn.: Interaction Book Company; Kouzes, J. M., & B. Z. Posner. (1987). *The leadership challenge.* San Francisco: Jossey-Bass; Kraut, A. I., P. R. Pedigo, D. D. McKenna, & M. D. Dunnette. (1989). The role of the manager: What's really important in different management jobs. *Academy of Management Executive* 3: 286–93.

11. Tjosvold, D., M. M. Tjosvold, & J. Tjosvold. (1991). *Love & anger: Managing family conflict.* Minneapolis: Team Media.

Chapter 4

1. Hackman, J. R., & R. E. Walton. Leading groups in organizations. In *Designing effective work groups,* ed. P. S. Goodman. San Francisco: Jossey-Bass, 72–119.

2. Kouzes, J. M., & B. Z. Posner. (1987). *The leadership challenge.* San Francisco: Jossey-Bass.

3. Congor, J. A. (1989). Leadership: The art of empowering others. *Academy of Management Review* 3: 17–24.

4. Argyris, C. (1970). *Intervention theory and method: A behavioral science view.* Reading, Mass.; Addison-Wesley.

Chapter 6

1. Johnson, D. W., R. T. Johnson, & E. J. Holubec. (1986). *Circles of learning.* Edina, Minn.: Interaction Book Company.

2. Johnson, D. W. & R. T. Johnson. (1989). *Cooperation and competition: Theory and research.* Edina, Minn.: Interaction Book Company.

3. Tjosvold, D. (1985). Implications of controversy research for management. *Journal of Management* 11: 21–37; Tjosvold, D. (1987). Participation: A close look at its dynamics. *Journal of Management* 13: 739–50.

4. Johnson, D. W. & R. T. Johnson. (1989b). *Leading the cooperative school.* Edina, Minn.: Interaction Book Company.

Chapter 7

1. Hammer, T. H. (1988). New developments in profit sharing, gainsharing, and employee ownership. In *Productivity in organizations: New perspectives from industrial and organizational psychology,* ed. J.P. Campbell & R.J. Campbell. San Francisco: Jossey-Bass, 328–66.
2. Kochan, T. A. & H. C. Katz. (1988). *Collective bargaining and industrial relations. From theory to policy and practice.* Homewood, Ill.: Irwin.
3. Banas, P. A. (1988). Employee involvement: A sustained labor/management initiative at the Ford Motor Company. In *Productivity in organizations: New perspectives from industrial and organizational psychology,* ed. J. P. Campbell & R. J. Campbell. San Francisco: Jossey-Bass, 388–416; Jusela, G. E., P. Chairman, R. A. Ball, C. E. Tyson, & K. D. Dannermiller. Work innovations at Ford Motor. In *Quality productivity and innovation: Strategies for gaining competitive advantage,* ed. Y.K. Shetty & V. M. Buehler. New York: Elsevier, 123–45.
4. Angle, H. L., & J. L. Perry. (1986). Dual commitment and labor-management relationship climates. *Academy of Management Journal* 29: 31–50; Magennau, J.M., J.E. Martin, & M.M. Peterson. (1988). Dual and unilateral commitment among stewards and rank-and-file union members. *Academy of Management Journal* 31: 359–76.
5. Kochan, T. A. (1980). *Collective bargaining and industrial relations.* Homewood, Ill.: Irwin; Kochan, T. A. & H. C. Katz. (1988). *Collective bargaining and industrial relations. From theory to policy and practice.* Homewood, Ill.: Irwin.
6. Morishima, M. (1991). Information sharing and firm performance in Japan *Industrial Relations: A Journal of Economy & Society,* 30: 37–61.
7. Morishima, M. (1991). Information sharing and collective bargaining in Japan: Effects of wage negotiation. *Industrial & Labor Relations Review,* 44: 469–85.
8. Katz, H. C., T. A. Kochan, & K. R. Gobeille. (1983) Industrial relations performance, economic performance, and QWL programs: An interplant analysis. *Industrial and Labor Relations Review* 37: 3–17; Katz, H. C., T. A. Kochan, & M. R. Weber. (1985). Assessing the effects of industrial relations systems and efforts to improve the quality of working life on organizational effectiveness. *Academy of Management Journal* 28: 509–26.
9. Becker, B. E. (1988). Concession bargaining: The meaning of union gains. *Academy of Management Journal* 31: 377–87.
10. Chase, R. B., & D. A. Garvin. (1989). The service factory. *Harvard Business Review* (July-August): 61–69.
11. Bushe, G., & A. Shani. (1990). *Parallel learning structures.* Reading, Mass.: Addison-Wesley; Pasmore, W. W., & F. Friedlander. (1982). An action-research program for increasing employee involvement in problem-solving. *Administrative Science Quarterly* 27: 343–62.

Chapter 9

1. Schwenk, C. R. (1984). Cognitive simplification processes in strategic decision-making. *Strategic Management Journal* 5: 111–28.
2. Cosier, R. A. (1978). The effects of three potential aids for making strategic decisions on prediction accuracy. *Organizational Behavior and Human Performance* 22: 295–306; Cosier, R. A., & C. R. Schwenk. (1990). Agreement and thinking alike: Ingredients for poor decisions. *Academy of Management Executive* 4: 69–74; George, A. (1974). Adaptation to stress in political decision-making: The individual, small group, and organizational contexts. In *Coping and adaptation,* ed. G.V. Coelho, D. A. Hamburg, & J.E. Adams. New York; Basic Books. 115–144; Johnson, D. W., R. T. Johnson, K. Smith, & D. Tjosvold. (1990). Pro, con, and synthesis: Training managers to engage in constructive controversy. *Research in negotiations in organization,* vol. 2, ed. B. Sheppard, M. Bazerman, & R. Lewicki. Greenwich, Conn.: JAI Press, 139–74; Mason, R. O., & I. I. Mitroff. (1981). *Challenging strategic planning assumptions.* New York: Wiley; Schweiger, D.M., W.R. Sandberg, & J. W. Ragan. (1986). Group approaches for improving strategic decision making: A comparative analysis of dialectical inquiry, devil's advocacy, and consensus. *Academy of Management Journal* 29: 51–71; Schweiger, D.M., W.R., Sandberg, & P.L. Rechner. (1989). Experimental effects of dialectical inquiry, devil's advocacy, and consensus approaches to strategic decision making. *Academy of Management Journal* 32: 745–72; Tjosvold, D. (1985). Implications of controversy research for management. *Journal of Management* 11: 21–37.
3. Johnson, D.W., & R.T. Johnson. (1989b). *Leading the cooperative school.* Edina, Minn.: Interaction Book Company.
4. Lewin, K. (1943). *Forces behind food habits and methods of change: The problem of changing food habits.* (NRC Bulletin No. 108). Washington, D.C.: National Research Council: Committee on Food Habits.
5. Janis, I., & L. Mann. (1977). *Decision-making: A psychological analysis of conflict, choice and commitment.* New York: Free Press.
6. Charkravarthy, B. S. (1984). Strategic self-renewal: A planning framework for today. *Academy of Management Review* 9: 536–47; Porter, M. (1985). *Competitive advantage.* New York: Free Press.
7. Anderson, P. A. (1983). Decision making by objection and the Cuban Missile Crisis. *Administrative Science Quarterly* 28: 201–222.
8. Eisenhardt, K.M. & L.J., Bourgeois, III. (1988). Politics of strategic decision making in high-velocity environments: Toward a midrange theory. *Academy of Management Journal* 31: 737–70.

Chapter 10

1. Little J. (1982). Norms of collegiality and experimentation: Workplace conditions for school success. *American Educational Research Journal* 19: 325–40.

2. Johnson, D.W., & R.T. Johnson. (1989b). *Leading the cooperative school.* Edina, Minn.: Interaction Book Company.
3. Ibid.

Chapter 11

1. U.S. Department of Commerce. (1985). *U.S. direct investment abroad, 1982: The benchmark survey.* Washington, D.C.: U.S. Government Printing Office.
2. Contractor, F.J., & Lorange, P. (1988). Why should firms cooperate? The strategy and economics basis for cooperative ventures. In *Cooperative strategies in international business,* ed. F. J. Contractor & P. Lorange. Lexington, Mass.: Lexington Books, 3–30.
3. Reich, R. B. (1984). Japan, Inc., U.S.A. *New Republic,* 26 November, 19–23.
4. Harrigan, K. (1985). *Strategies for joint ventures.* Lexington, Mass.: Lexington Books. Holton, R. H. (1981). Making international joint ventures work. In *The management of headquarters subsidiary relations in multinational corporations,* ed. L. Otterbeck. London: Gower, 255–67.
5. Shekar, O., & Y. Zeira. (1990). International joint ventures: A tough test for HR. *Personnel* (January): 26–31; Shekar, O., & Y. Zeira. (1987). Human resources management in international joint ventures: Directions for research. *Academy of Management Review* 12, 546–57.
6. Krantz, K. T. (1989). How Velcro got hooked on quality. *Harvard Business Review* (September-October): 34–39.

Index

Ad hoc decision-making groups, 82–83
Advocacy teams, for making decisions,
    138–140
  and constructive controversy, 140
  guides for, 140
Allen-Bradley, 97
Alternatives, evaluation of, 115–116,
    135
Assessment: *See* Reflection
Attitudes, changing, 67
Authority
  and cooperative approach, 35–36
  leaders' problems with, 32–33, 35–36
  and pitfalls to avoid, 33–34

Boss management, 36–37, 179
Brainstorming, and constructive contro-
    versy, 134

Change
  as cooperative goal, 36–37, 115
  principles of, 172
  steps for developing, 173–174
Competitive-individualistic climates
  rationales for, 20–22
  short-term advantages of, 24
  and the status quo, 24
  See also Individualistic climates
Competitive outdoing/striving, 1–3
  short-term advantages of, 2–3
Concession bargaining, use of, 95
Consensus, as problem-solving method,
    136–137
Consultation, 55, 95
Controversy, constructive
  and advocacy teams, 140–141
  and brainstorming, 134–135
  and consensus, 136
  as contribution to teamwork, 52–53,
    55, 67, 68

guidelines for encouraging, 53–54,
    183–184
  and pitfalls to avoid, 184
  See also Problem-solving, and explor-
    ing opposing views
Cooperative leadership, 34–36
Cooperative relationship, 34–36, 95,
    98–99
Cooperative ventures
  advantages of, 160–161
  of General Electric, 161
  between General Motors and Toyota,
    164–165
  management challenges posed by,
    161–162
  risks of, 161–162
  structuring of, 162–164
Customers, consultation with, 95–96,
    166

Decision making, 52–53, 135–137
  ad hoc groups for, 82–83
  advocacy teams for, 138–140

Employees
  cooperative relationships among,
    94–95
  and hierarchy of power and authority,
    32–33
  and managing the boss, 36–37, 179
  and misconceptions about leadership,
    33
  reaching out to, 85–91
  and self-protection, 32, 33
  structuring relationships among, 37
  See also Employee teams
Employee teams, 101–113
  empowerment of, 117–118
  and exploring issues, 118
  guides for developing, 182–183
  and pitfalls to avoid, 183

Employee teams (*cont.*)
  and reflection, 118
  unity of, 117
  visions and goals of, 116–117
  See also Project teams
Empowerment, 6, 14–15, 44, 49–50
  steps toward, 50–52, 117–118

Feedback, 115, 148–149
  guides for observing and giving, 149
Force field analysis, in problem-solving,
  132–133

General Electric, and cooperative ventures of, 161
General Motors
  joint venture with Toyota, 164–165
  partnership with Velcro, 166–167
Global competition, 157–160
  and cooperative ventures, 160–161
  See also Partnerships across organizations

Helmreich, Robert, 30–31
Hewlett-Packard, 97

Improvements, how to make, 54–57
Individualistic climates, limits of,
  113–114; *see also* Competitive-
  individualistic climates
Industrial relations
  as a competitive advantage, 94–95
  from a Marxist perspective, 92
  from a mixed-motive perspective, 92
  from a unitarian perspective, 92
Information sharing, 55
  in Japanese firms, 95
Innovation
  steps toward, 114–116
  and the team organization model,
  116–118

Japanese firms
  and cooperative ventures, 161
  and General Motors and Toyota joint
  venture, 164–165
  and innovation, 96
  and reducing labor costs, 114
  and use of information sharing, 95
Jigsawing method, of understanding the
  team organization model, 81–82
Joint ventures: *See* Cooperative ventures

Labor: *See* Unions
Leader development teams, 143–146
  activities of, 148–149
  goals and attitudes of, 147–148
  guides for developing, 149, 153–154
  and pitfalls to avoid, 185
  steps for constructing, 150–153, 154–
  155, 185
Leaders
  competitiveness of, 30–31
  empowerment of, 146–147
  misconceptions of, xi–xii, 33
  myths about, 30–31
  power and authority of, 32–33
  See also Team organization leader
Leadership, 11–19, 27–30
  ambiguities of, 22, 37–38
  and barriers to leading the team organization, 19–23
  and creating productive work relationships, 31–38
  employees' misconceptions about, 33
  guides for confronting, 177
  and pitfalls to avoid, 33–34, 177–178
  requirements of, 27–30
  See also Cooperative leadership

Management, and team organization
  model, 61–69; *see also* Middle
  managers
Marxist industrial relations, 92
Middle managers
  and conflict with unions, 86–91
  guides for reaching out to, 180
  and pitfalls to avoid, 180–181
  and supervisors, 71–80

Organizations: *See* Global competition;
  Partnerships across organizations

Partnerships across organizations,
  157–160
  guides for structuring, 186
  and pitfalls to avoid, 186
  See also Global competition
Power
  leaders' problems with, 32–33
  and the cooperative relationship,
  35–36
Problem-solving
  and exploring opposing views,
  129–131

guides for developing teams for, 184
and pitfalls to avoid, 185
steps for, 131–138
See also Controversy, constructive
Project teams, 123–129; *see also* Employee teams

Reflection, 7, 54–57
methods of, 56–57, 118
Reingold, Edwin, ix
Relationships
cooperative 17–18, 34–35, 95, 98–99
structuring, among employees, 37
value of, 17, 23–24
in the workplace, 17, 31–37

Singlemindedness, on tasks, 20, 113–114
Solutions
creating, 133–138
implementing and monitoring, 137–138
proposing, 137
Status quo, 23–24, 55, 82

Task singlemindedness: *See* Singlemindedness, on tasks
Task forces: *See* Project teams; Employee teams
Team building, 80–81
Team organization
advantages of, 5
attitudes in, 3–4
components of, 44–45
development of, 169–172, 174–175
guides for, 179, 182
management and, 61–66
obstacles in leading, 19–23
and pitfalls to avoid, 180, 182
Team organization leader
attitudes and goals of, 5–7

guides for, 178
and pitfalls to avoid, 178
Team organization model, 4, 39–44, 42–44, 68–69
as an alternative to union-management conflict, 92–93
and innovation, 116–118
and jigsawing method, 81–82
Teamwork
attitudes of, 1, 44–45
as approach of team organization, 4
and change, 172
and jigsawing method, 81–82
in the service factory, 96–98
and team building, 80–81
and technology, 97–98
and voicing ambiguities, 66–67
See also Employee teams; Project teams
Toyota, joint venture with General Motors, 164–165

Unions
and conflicts with management, 85–91, 92–93
contribution of, 93
guides for working with, 181
and pitfalls to avoid, 181–182
reaching out to, 85–91
and the team organization model, 92–94
Unity
among coworkers, 5–6, 47
across organizations, 164–165
guidelines for, 47–49

Velcro, partnership with General Motors, 166–167
Visions, 5, 45, 116–117
shared, ways of creating, 45–47

Workers: *See* Employees; Unions

About the Authors

After graduating from Princeton University, **Dean Tjosvold** earned his Ph.D. in the social psychology of organizations at the University of Minnesota in 1972 and is now a professor on the Faculty of Business Administration at Simon Fraser University, Burnaby, B.C. He has also taught at Pennsylvania State University and was a visiting scholar at the National University of Singapore and at the University of Gröningen in the Netherlands. He has published over 100 articles on managing conflict, cooperation and competition, decision making, power, and other management issues. With David W. Johnson he edited *Productive Conflict Management: Perspectives for Organizations* (Irvington: New York, 1983) and with Mary Tjosvold has written books for health care professionals and for families. He also wrote *Working Together to Get Things Done: Managing for Organizational Productivity* (Lexington Books, 1986) and has recently published *Team Organization: An Enduring Competitive Advantage* (Wiley & Sons, 1991), as part of the Industrial and Organizational Psychology Series, and *The Conflict-Positive Organization: Stimulate Diversity and Create Unity* (Addison-Wesley, 1991), as part of the Organizational Development Series. He consults on conflict management and related issues in diverse companies and is a partner in several family businesses in Minnesota.

Mary Tjosvold earned her Ph.D. in educational administration from the University of Minnesota in 1975 and also completed the owner/president management program at the Harvard Business School in 1987. She developed and is now a partner in Camilia Rose Convalescent Center and Group Home, Six Acres Townhouses, DeMar Children's Home, Margaret Place Apartments for Elderly, and other facilities. She founded and is CEO of Mary T. Inc. which manages these and other residential and social services in Minnesota with annual revenues of $10 million. Previously, she taught in Illinois and Minnesota and served as an educational consultant. She has published extensively on management, productive conflict, and sex bias. She authored, with Dean Tjosvold, *Working with Mentally Handicapped Persons in Their Residences* (Free Press, 1981), *Working with Elderly in Their Residences* (Praeger, 1983), and *Love & Anger: Managing Family Conflict* (Team Media, 1991).

She is very active in community and educational affairs, serving on a wide variety of task forces and agencies and is an articulate advocate and supporter of women in business. She has given presentations and conducted workshops on productive conflict, cooperation and competition, entrepreneurship, managing diversity, and other human resource issues for clients in various industries. She has been recognized in several publications as a leading Minnesotan business woman, advocate, and speaker.